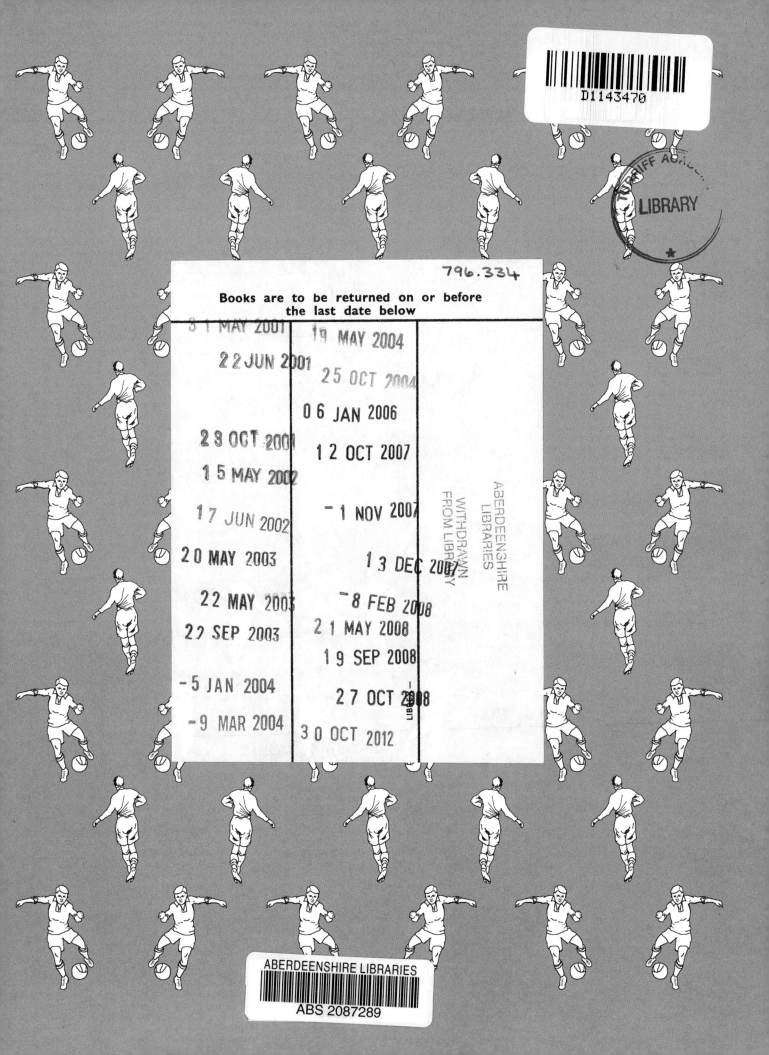

FOOTBALL

1930s French hair-oil advertisement

DON DU
GRAND MATCH
D'ASSOCIATION

1905 match holder

1900s football pumps

Jay Jay Okacha of Nigeria

1900s shinpads

1910s shinpads

1930s shinpads

Early 20th-century football stencils

1966 World Cup football

1998 World Cup football

1930s painting of a goalkeeper

Porcelain
figure

Porcelain
figure

FOOTBALL

Written by
HUGH HORNBY

Photographed by
ANDY CRAWFORD

1912 football

Dorling Kindersley
in association with
THE FOOTBALL MUSEUM

19th-century jersey

1900s plaster figure

DK

Dorling Kindersley
LONDON, NEW YORK, DELHI,
JOHANNESBURG, MUNICH, PARIS, and SYDNEY

For a full catalogue, visit

DK www.dk.com

Project editor Louise Pritchard
Art editor Jill Plank
Assistant editor Annabel Blackledge
Assistant art editor Yolanda Belton
Managing editor Sue Grabham
Senior managing art editor Julia Harris
Production Kate Oliver
Picture research Amanda Gregory
DTP Designer Andrew O'Brien and Georgia Bryer

This Eyewitness ® Guide has been conceived by
Dorling Kindersley Limited and Editions Gallimard

First published in Great Britain in 2000
by Dorling Kindersley Limited,
9 Henrietta Street, London WC2E 8PS

2 4 6 8 10 9 7 5 3 1

A CIP catalogue record for this book is
available from the British Library.

ISBN 0-7513-6217-4

Colour reproduction by Colourscan, Singapore
Printed in China by Toppan Printing Co. (Shenzhen) Ltd.

1925 Australian
International shirt

1908 Newcastle shirt

1905 book cover image

1940s whistle

THE REFEREE

Early 20th-century snap card

1895 penknife

1900 penknife

1900s silver match holder

1930s silver hatpin

1920s silver flint lighter

Shirts from 1890s catalogue

Contents

Hungary badge

Holland badge

Italy badge

Brazil badge

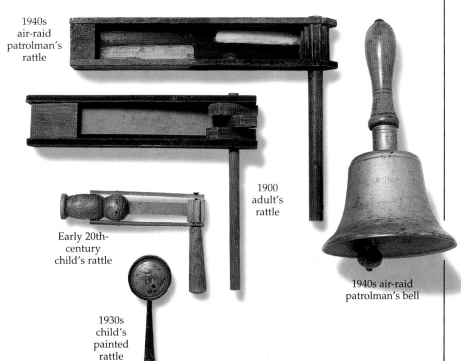
1940s air-raid patrolman's rattle

1900 adult's rattle

Early 20th-century child's rattle

1930s child's painted rattle

1940s air-raid patrolman's bell

The global game

FOOTBALL HAS ITS ROOTS IN ancient China, Europe, and the Americas. People kicked a ball to prepare for war, to honour their gods, or just to entertain themselves. For centuries, different versions of ball-kicking games existed. In Europe, they were tests of courage and strength and in China and other Eastern countries, the games were rituals of grace and skill. The rules of the modern game of football were not drawn up until 1863 but the qualities that we admire in it – speed, agility, bravery, and spirit – have been present in many cultures for more than 2,000 years.

An Ashbourne ball

ASHBOURNE BALL
Ashbourne in Derbyshire, England is the site of one of several traditional Shrove Tuesday football games. It is characterized by disorder. Two teams, the Upwards and the Downwards, try to move the ball through the opposition's "goal" – a gateway at the other end of town.

HARROW BALL
English public schools, including Harrow and Eton, played a crucial role in developing modern football in the early 1800s. Although each school played the game differently, they all produced detailed, written rules. These provided the basis for the first official laws.

The Harrow ball was flattened, top and bottom.

FOOTBALL TRAINING
The Chinese were playing a type of football by the 3rd century BC. A military book of that period refers to *tsu chu,* or "kicking a ball". The game may once have been part of a soldier's training and was later included in ceremonies on the emperor's birthday.

These symbols were once described by an official of the English Football Association as "To kick with the foot"

Chinese characters meaning "football"

A GENTLEMEN'S GAME
The game of calcio was played in Italian cities such as Venice and Florence in the 16th and 17th centuries. On certain festival days, two teams of gentlemen would attempt to force the ball through openings at either end of a city square. Although physical contact was a feature of calcio, the game also had a tactical element. Teams used formations and attempted to create space in which to advance.

Local people came out to watch the games

Handling the ball was part of the game

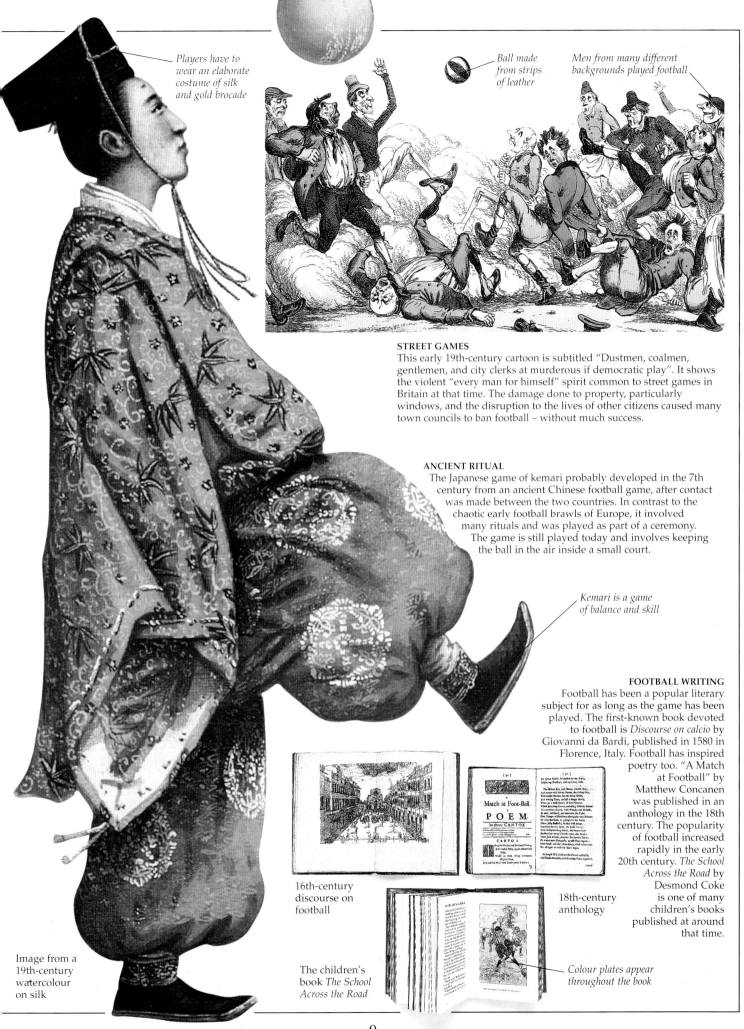

Players have to
wear an elaborate
costume of silk
and gold brocade

Ball made
from strips
of leather

Men from many different
backgrounds played football

STREET GAMES

This early 19th-century cartoon is subtitled "Dustmen, coalmen, gentlemen, and city clerks at murderous if democratic play". It shows the violent "every man for himself" spirit common to street games in Britain at that time. The damage done to property, particularly windows, and the disruption to the lives of other citizens caused many town councils to ban football – without much success.

ANCIENT RITUAL

The Japanese game of kemari probably developed in the 7th century from an ancient Chinese football game, after contact was made between the two countries. In contrast to the chaotic early football brawls of Europe, it involved many rituals and was played as part of a ceremony. The game is still played today and involves keeping the ball in the air inside a small court.

Kemari is a game
of balance and skill

FOOTBALL WRITING

Football has been a popular literary subject for as long as the game has been played. The first-known book devoted to football is *Discourse on calcio* by Giovanni da Bardi, published in 1580 in Florence, Italy. Football has inspired poetry too. "A Match at Football" by Matthew Concanen was published in an anthology in the 18th century. The popularity of football increased rapidly in the early 20th century. *The School Across the Road* by Desmond Coke is one of many children's books published at around that time.

16th-century
discourse on
football

18th-century
anthology

Image from a
19th-century
watercolour
on silk

The children's
book *The School
Across the Road*

Colour plates appear
throughout the book

9

History of football

THE GAME THAT HAS CAPTURED the imagination of people all over the world was developed in England and Scotland in the 19th century. The former pupils of English public schools produced the first common set of rules and formed the Football Association (FA) in 1863. Things moved forwards quickly. British administrators, merchants, and engineers took the game overseas and people from other countries began to play football. The first international matches were followed by professional leagues and big competitions.

CELEBRITY PLAYER
The first footballers were amateurs. C B Fry, who played for the Corinthians in the late 1890s, was one of the first football celebrities. He was also a member of the England cricket team and held the world long-jump record.

Arnold Kirke Smith's cap

EXHIBITIONISM
Throughout the early years of the 20th century, British teams toured the world, introducing football to other countries by playing exhibition matches. This shield was presented to the Islington Corinthians in Japan, in 1937.

Kinnaird once did a headstand after winning a Cup final

The English Three Lions motif was first used in 1872

Arnold Kirke Smith's England shirt

The shirt is made of closely woven wool

THE FIRST INTERNATIONAL
In November 1872, Scotland played England on a cricket field in Glasgow in the first ever international match. About 2,000 spectators watched a 0–0 draw. This shirt and cap were worn by Arnold Kirke Smith from Oxford University, who was a member of the English team.

MODERN RULES
Lord Kinnaird was President of the Football Association from 1890–1923, and was one of the amateurs who shaped the rules and structure of the modern game. Previously, he had played in nine of the first 12 FA Cup finals, winning five.

TALENTED TEAMS
The English Football League began in 1888. Its 12-team fixture programme was inspired by US baseball. This picture by Thomas Hemy shows two successful clubs of the 1890s: Aston Villa who won the league five times and Sunderland, "the team of all talents", who won three times.

THE UNRULY GAME

The first French football league, set up in 1894, was dominated by teams of Scottish emigrants, such as the White Rovers and Standard AC. French satirists were quick to refer to the game's reputation for unruliness. This 1900s French magazine, *Le Monde Comique*, reflects this attitude towards the game.

Bystanders often got caught up in the boisterous action

Cover illustration entitled *"Les Plaisirs du Dimanche"* ("Sunday Pleasures")

In reality, women's kit was far less figure-hugging

A ball of exaggerated size

LADIES FIRST

Women's football started at the end of the 19th century. Teams such as the British Ladies' Club attracted large crowds. During the First World War, men's and women's teams played against each other for charity. The first women's World Cup was held in China in 1991 and was won by the USA.

FIFA badge

FORMING FIFA

By 1904, several countries, including France, Belgium, Denmark, the Netherlands, Spain, Sweden, and Switzerland had their own administrators. They formed the world governing body, FIFA (Fédération Internationale de Football Associations). By 1939, more than 50 countries had joined.

This 1900s plaster figure is wearing shin-pads that were typical of that time

Ugandan batik

Each stamp shows a different US player

US stamps produced for the 1994 World Cup

OUT OF AFRICA

Football spread through Africa from both ends of the continent. South Africa, with its European populations, was an obvious foothold and sent a touring party to South America in 1906. In 1923, Egypt, in North Africa, were the first African team to join FIFA.

SOCCER

Youth soccer is the most widely played sport in the USA, for both boys and girls. The 1994 World Cup provided a big boost for Major League Soccer, which is bringing top-level professional games to a new audience. The USA reached the semi-finals of the very first World Cup in 1930.

Laws of the game

THE RULES OF A GAME should be brief and easy to understand. It is certain that football's success has been partly due to the simplicity of its Laws. Rules governing equipment, the pitch, foul play, and restarts have all survived the passage of time. Football has always been a free-flowing game. Stoppages can be avoided if the referee uses the advantage rule – allowing play to continue after a foul, providing that the right team still has the ball. The offside rule has always been a source of controversy in the game. The assistant referees have to make split-second decisions about whether an attacker has strayed beyond the second last defender at the moment the ball is played forwards by one of his or her team-mates. A player cannot be offside from a throw-in.

STAND BACK
This throw-in is illegal. The ball is held correctly in both hands but the feet, though they are both on the ground as they should be, are over the line.

There have been goal posts since the early days of football but, until the crossbar was introduced in 1875, tape was stretched between them 2.5 m (8 ft) from the ground

The penalty spot is 12 yd (11 m) from the goal-line

Goal kicks must be taken from within the 6-yd (5.5-m) box

Players must not cross the half-way line until the ball is kicked off

PENALTY
Penalties were introduced in 1891 as a punishment for foul play, such as tripping, pushing, or handball in the 18-yd (16.5-m) box. A player takes a shot at goal from the penalty spot with only the goalkeeper to beat. If the ball rebounds from the post or bar the penalty taker cannot play it again before someone else has touched it.

FREE KICK
There are two types of free kick – direct and indirect. In an indirect free kick, awarded after an infringement of a Law, the ball must be touched by two players before a goal is scored. Direct free kicks are given after fouls and the taker may score immediately. Opposing players must be at least 10 yd (9 m) away from the ball at a free kick.

CORNER
A corner kick is taken when the defending team puts the ball out of play behind their own goal-line. Corner kicks provide useful goal-scoring opportunities. The ball must be placed within the quadrant – a quarter circle with a radius of 1 yd (1 m) in the corner of the pitch. A goal can be scored directly from a corner kick.

FAKING FOULS
The amateur footballers of the 19th century believed that all fouls were accidental and would have been horrified by the "professional foul", an offence deliberately committed to prevent an attack from developing. Unfortunately, the game today is full of deliberate fouls. Some players also fake being fouled to win their team a free kick.

When a penalty is taken, only the taker is allowed inside the "D"

CHARGE!
The 1958 English FA Cup final between Manchester United and Bolton Wanderers is remembered for the disputed goal scored by Bolton's centre-forward, Nat Lofthouse. He charged the United goalkeeper, Harry Gregg, over the line as he caught the ball – a challenge that all referees today would consider a foul.

Players from the defending team must stay out of the 10-yd (9-m) circle before the kick-off

Players cannot be offside in their own half of the pitch

The 6-yd (5.5-m) and 18-yd (16.5-m) boxes were semi-circular until 1902

A goalkeeper is restricted to four steps when kicking a ball out of the hands

Assistant referees patrol opposite sides of the field and cover one half each, their main responsibilities being to signal throw-ins and flag for offside

PERMANENT MARKERS
In the mid 19th century, before it was stipulated that permanent lines should be marked on the pitch, flags were used as a guide to whether the ball was out of play. Today, a corner flag has to be at least 5 ft (1.5 m) high to avoid the risk of players being impaled.

LAW AND ORDER
There are 17 main football Laws. The field of play must be rectangular and, for a full-size pitch, from 110 to 120 yd (100.5 to 110 m) long and from 70 to 80 yds (64 to 73 m) wide. There should be 11 players per side. Substitution rules have changed over the years and teams may now substitute any three from five players, including the goalie, during stoppages in the match. The duration of play is 90 minutes, in two halves of 45 minutes each.

Goal nets were first manufactured by Brodies of Liverpool, England, in 1891 and welcomed as a means of settling disputes over whether a ball had actually entered the goal

The referee

EARLY AMATEUR players put a high value on fair play but saw the need for officials on the football pitch. To begin with, each team provided an umpire from their own club, who did not interfere much with the passage of play. At this stage, players had to raise an arm and appeal for a decision if they felt that they had been fouled, otherwise play continued. The rise of professional football in the 1880s made it harder for umpires to be neutral. A referee was introduced to settle disputes. In 1891, the referee was moved on to the field of play and the umpires became linesmen, a system that has continued ever since. Linesmen and women, are now called assistant referees.

Early 20th century snap card caricature of a referee

YOUR NUMBER'S UP
One duty of the assistant referees is to control the entrance of substitutes to the field, checking their studs and indicating with number cards which player is to be replaced. At top levels of the game, a fourth official uses an illuminated board to indicate substitutes and inform everyone how much injury time will be played at the end of each half.

CLASSIC BLACK
This is the classic referee's uniform, all black with white cuffs and collar. Dating from the 1970s, this kit is similar to all those worn after the phasing out of the blazer in the 1940s to the introduction of other colours in the 1990s. The bulky jackets of the early 1900s were replaced by a less constricting shirt to encourage the officials to keep up with play on the pitch.

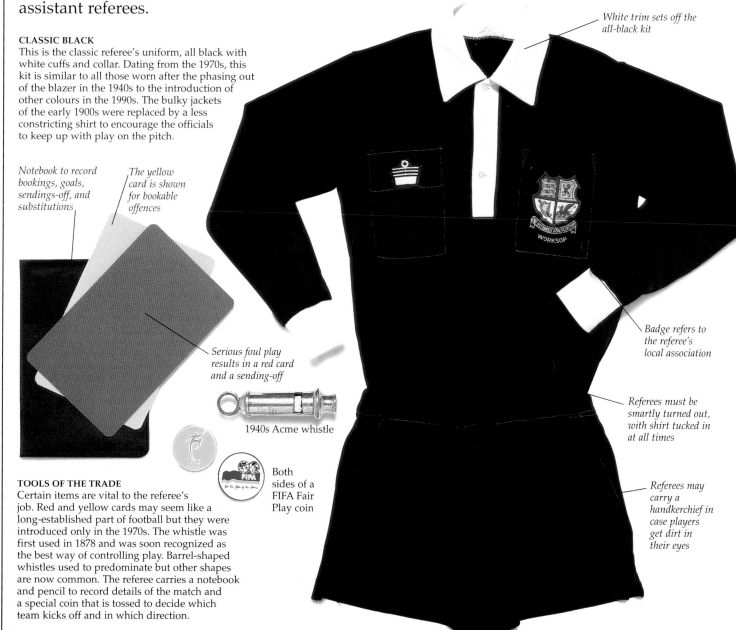

White trim sets off the all-black kit

Notebook to record bookings, goals, sendings-off, and substitutions

The yellow card is shown for bookable offences

Serious foul play results in a red card and a sending-off

1940s Acme whistle

Both sides of a FIFA Fair Play coin

Badge refers to the referee's local association

Referees must be smartly turned out, with shirt tucked in at all times

Referees may carry a handkerchief in case players get dirt in their eyes

TOOLS OF THE TRADE
Certain items are vital to the referee's job. Red and yellow cards may seem like a long-established part of football but they were introduced only in the 1970s. The whistle was first used in 1878 and was soon recognized as the best way of controlling play. Barrel-shaped whistles used to predominate but other shapes are now common. The referee carries a notebook and pencil to record details of the match and a special coin that is tossed to decide which team kicks off and in which direction.

YOU'RE BOOKED
Bookings used to be given only once or twice per match and sendings-off were extremely rare, but FIFA now insist that referees are much stricter. As a result, teams regularly have to play with 10 team members, or even fewer.

A red card is shown when a player has committed two bookable offences

Former USSR

Australia

New Zealand

Bangladesh

Iceland

Portugal

USA

Columbia

Italy

Cards are produced with a flourish from this pocket

WORLD-CLASS REFEREES
These badges are produced by Referees' Associations around the world. Despite all the abuse they receive, referees are motivated by the prospect of officiating at top-class games. World Cup matches are controlled by officials from all countries affiliated to FIFA, not just those that qualify as competitors.

LINESMAN FIFA 92

LINESWOMAN FIFA 95

Official FIFA badges for sewing on the officials' shirts

Men and women officiate at top-level football matches

The referee times the game with a watch

TOUCHLINE HELPERS
The first linesmen waved a handkerchief to alert the referee. Assistant referees today use a flag. They wave the flag when a player is off-side, when the ball is out of play, and when they have seen an infringement on the pitch.

Referees have to be fit to keep up with play on the pitch

The first referees wore plus-two trousers

Blazer with pockets for a stopwatch and notebook

HOW TO BE A REFEREE
This illustration from the cover of a 1906 book entitled *How to be a Referee* shows the typical referee's clothing of that period. After taking a qualifying exam, referees usually start out at amateur level. They are assessed regularly to ensure that standards remain high. Eventually, after years of experience, referees may progress to officiate at international tournaments.

The pitch

This Samuel Brandão painting of Rio de Janeiro shows football being played on bare earth.

A<small>T THE START OF A SEASON</small>, footballers can look forward to playing their first match on a smooth green pitch. If a pitch is not looked after, it soon becomes muddy and uneven, especially if cold, wet weather sets in.

Patterns can be made when mowing the pitch

Groundstaff try to keep the pitches in good condition with the help of new species of grass and good drainage. In many northern European countries, football takes a mid-winter break during the worst conditions. Wealthy clubs may lay a completely new pitch between matches, but millions of amateur players have to make do with whatever muddy or frozen land is available.

STREETS AHEAD
In the days before traffic became too heavy, street football was a popular pastime. Children learned close ball control and dribbling skills in confined spaces. They often used heaps of clothes or gateways as goalposts.

Jean-Pierre Papin playing for AC Milan, Italy, on a snow-covered pitch

Groundstaff preparing for a match during the 1953 English season

PLAYING IN SNOW
In snowy weather, the pitch markings and the white football are hard to see and the ground is slippery. If the markings can be swept clear and the pitch is soft enough to take a stud, play can usually carry on, using a more visible orange ball.

HOT STUFF
In countries where the weather is cold during the football season, many methods have been tried to prevent pitches from freezing. Undersoil heating was first installed in England at Everton in 1958. Before undersoil heating became common, ground staff put straw down as insulation and lit fires in braziers to lift the air temperature. Today, large covers are sometimes used to protect pitches.

SLOPES AND SHADE

Modern pitches are usually laid with a camber, which means that they slope slightly down from the centre circle to the touchlines. This helps to drain water away. When large stands are built, less air and light reach the grass, stunting its growth. This has been a problem at some stadiums, such as the San Siro in Milan, Italy.

PAMPERING THE PITCH

Modern pitch maintenance is a full-time job. In the summer, the grass must be mowed, watered, and fed regularly. During the close season, work is done to repair holes and worn patches in the turf. New types of grass have been developed that grow better in the shade of tall stands. This is vital in helping the ground staff to keep the pitch in good condition.

The surface is made to mimic grass

Fibres are woven together to form a carpet

Artificial grass viewed from the side, top, and underneath

Grass is kept long to encourage deep rooting

Layer of top-soil nourishes the grass

Heating pipes laid in grids

Layers of sand and gravel allow water to filter away

The base of the pitch is composed of large pieces of stone

Drainage pipes carry away water

Model of a section through a pitch

BETTER THAN THE REAL THING?

Artificial pitches are made from synthetic turf laid on a shock-absorbent pad. They are more hard-wearing than grass pitches and are unaffected by torrential rain or freezing cold. Clubs with an artificial pitch can rent out their stadium for a range of events, such as pop concerts, and their home matches need never be postponed because of bad weather. Many players do not like the surface because they feel that it increases the risk of injury.

SATURATION POINT

Rainwater is the greatest threat to pitch condition. Good built-in drainage is therefore an important part of pitch construction. Pipes and materials chosen for their good draining qualities are laid under the grass. A large amount of sand is mixed into the top-soil to make it less absorbent and less prone to becoming waterlogged. Even a well-cared-for pitch may become saturated. Ground staff sometimes have to resort to using garden forks to remove standing water.

Football skills

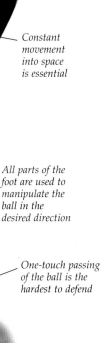

Early 20th-century button showing a man heading the ball

Each position on the field is associated with a specific range of tasks. Defenders must be able to tackle the opposition and claim the ball, midfielders need to pass the ball accurately to their team-mates, and strikers have to shoot and score goals. Although most players specialize in a certain position, professional players are expected to master a range of skills and work on any weaknesses. As part of their daily training routine, they practise hard to perfect their skills so that their technique does not let them down in a match.

CONTROL FREAK
Some of the most gifted players, such as Brazil's Roberto Carlos, are able to manipulate the ball with their feet, making it swerve, curl, or dip. This type of ball control helps them to bend passes around defenders and also to score from free kicks well outside the penalty area.

Shouting helps the players to pick each other out

TACKLE TALK
Players try to take the ball from another player by tackling. Lilian Thuram of France and Parma, Italy, is one of the world's great tacklers. He shows the timing and precision that are essential to avoid committing a foul. Referees punish players if they make a physical challenge from behind or if they make contact with a player instead of the ball.

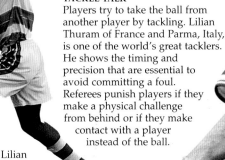

Lilian Thuram

Hand signals are used to improve teamwork

Constant movement into space is essential

PASS MARK
Moving the ball quickly around the pitch, from one player to another, is the most effective means of stretching a defence. Accurate passing remains the hallmark of all successful teams. Zinedine Zidane was the star of the 1998 World Cup final for France. He has the vision to pass the ball into space for his strikers even when he is tightly marked.

If the defender is unable to reach the ball, he must still challenge the striker

The player must time his leap to meet the ball firmly

Oliver Bierhoff

All parts of the foot are used to manipulate the ball in the desired direction

One-touch passing of the ball is the hardest to defend

HEADS UP!
There are two distinct kinds of heading – defensive and attacking. Defenders try to gain distance when they clear a high ball out of the goal area. Attackers need accuracy and power to score goals with a header. Oliver Bierhoff of Germany and Milan, Italy, is one of the best modern strikers in the air.

The ability to pass with both feet gives the player more options

Leaning back helps to ensure that the ball will rise towards the top of the net

GOING FOR GOAL
When shooting, forwards need the accuracy to find the corner of the net as well as the power to blast the ball through the defence. Gabriel Batistuta of Argentina beats goalkeepers regularly with his powerful right foot.

Keeping the head still improves accuracy

Keeping your weight over the ball makes it easier to cross with power

Extending the arms assists with balance

WINGING IT
Crosses, or passes in from the wings, result in more goals than any other angle of attack. Players who can put the ball over with pace and accuracy are extremely valuable to a team. David Beckham of Manchester United and England is renowned for the way he crosses from the right wing, curling the ball around the full-back and away from the goalkeeper. This type of swinging cross is often used when players are taking corners. They curl the ball in from the corner towards the goal and the waiting strikers.

The left leg is firmly planted to allow the body to make the best shape for the cross

The foot turns in as it passes through the ball to make it swerve

The player can feint to go in one direction before going in the other

The bicycle kick is even harder if the ball is moving across the player

BICYCLE KICK
The bicycle kick was first demonstrated in the 1930s by Brazilian forward Leonidas. It is one of the most difficult skills to pull off. With their back to the goal, strikers throw their legs up in the air and kick the ball while falling backwards. This tactic sometimes catches the goalkeeper by surprise. This model of Italian striker Roberto Baggio shows the ideal body position.

A higher jump allows the player to keep the ball down below the crossbar

DOWN-TOWN DRIBBLER
When a player runs with the ball at his feet, it is called dribbling. Brazilian star Ronaldo, who learned his football on the streets of Rio de Janeiro, is proof that dribbling can cause problems for the opposition. Good balance and concentration help a dribbler to change direction quickly and ride tackles.

The goalkeeper

A<small>S THE LAST LINE</small> of defence, a goalkeeper knows that a single mistake can cost the team victory. Goalkeeping can be a lonely job. It entails having different skills from the rest of the team and you can be unoccupied for several minutes at a time. The recent change to the back-pass law, forcing the goalkeeper to kick clear rather than pick up the ball, has made the job even harder. The necessity of having both a physical presence and great agility means that goalkeepers have to train harder than any other player, but the reward for this diligence can be a much longer career than that of their team-mates.

A 1900s Vesta, or match holder, showing a goalkeeper punching clear

Clothes

Until 1913, goalkeepers were distinguishable only by their cap, making it difficult for the referee to judge who, in a goalmouth scramble, was handling the ball. From 1913 to the early 1990s, they wore a shirt of a single plain colour that was different from the shirts worn by the rest of their team. A rule was made forbidding short sleeves which has now been relaxed.

GOOD SAVE
This 1950 comic cover shows the save that is considered to be the easiest to make – from a shot straight to the midriff. It also hints at the spectacular action in which goalkeepers are regularly involved, such as when they have to fly through the air to tip the ball away. Modern strikers are likely to make the ball swerve suddenly, so it is all the more important for goalies to keep their bodies in line with the ball.

CATCH IT
Punching the ball away from the danger area has always been popular among European and South American goalkeepers. The goalkeeper depicted on this 1900 book cover is trying to punch the ball but he probably should be trying to catch it because he is not being closely challenged. In the modern game, referees rarely allow goalkeepers to be charged when they are attempting to catch the ball.

The ball should be punched out towards the wing

KEEPERS' COLOURS
Patterns in football shirts have traditionally been limited to stripes and hoops but since the rules on goalkeepers' clothes were relaxed, every combination of colours seems to have been tried. Not all of them have been easy on the eye, although fluorescent designs are easy for defenders to see.

Flexible plastic ribs reinforce each finger

Modern gloves help to prevent injuries such as a broken finger

The shamrock, symbol of Ireland

EIRE SHIRT
This shirt was worn by Alan Kelly for the Republic of Ireland. He made 47 appearances, the first against West Germany in 1957 and the last against Norway in 1973. Yellow shirts were once a common sight in international matches. Green was not an option for the Irish goalkeeper because the strip of the Irish team is green.

GOALIE'S GLOVES
Until the 1970s, gloves were worn only when it was wet, and they were made of thin cotton. Modern goalkeepers wear gloves in all conditions. Various coatings and pads are used to increase the gloves' grip, which is the key to handling the ball.

NARROWING THE ANGLE
This image from the 1930s shows a goalkeeper alert to danger. When an attacker approaches the goal with the ball, goalkeepers should leave their line and move towards the ball to reduce the target area for the attacker. This "narrowing of the angle" is an important part of keepers' roles. They often make marks, in line with the posts, to help them keep their bearings when leaving the line.

Most goalkeepers may still wear a cap if the sun is in their eyes

Arms are outstretched, ready to block a shot

THROWING OUT
This painted button from the 1900s shows one of the goalkeeper's jobs. A quick throw out, particularly after catching a corner, can be an effective way of launching an attack. Some goalkeepers are renowned for the length of their throw.

GOAL KICK
When the ball is put out behind the goal-line by an attacker, the opposing team is awarded a goal kick. As shown on this button, the goalkeeper takes the kick from inside the 6-yard (5.5-m) box. When the ball was made of heavy leather, a goal kick rarely reached the opposition's half.

LOUD AND CLEAR
Peter Schmeichel is famous for the vehemence of his reaction when a team-mate makes a mistake. Here he is shouting at Roy Keane when playing for Manchester United, England. Although such eruptions risk undermining team spirit, it is far better for goalkeepers to communicate with their defenders than to be quiet. Goalies also have to shout when organizing the wall at free kicks.

Tactics

P ART OF FOOTBALL'S appeal is its tactical element. Coaches and managers try to outwit the opposition by keeping their tactics secret until the match. Since football first began, teams have lined up in different formations trying to play in a way that will take the other team by surprise and result in a goal. Early players had the physical attributes and skills needed for a particular position on the field. Today, the pace of the game demands that players are adaptable enough to play in almost any position, in the manner of the Dutch "total football" teams of the 1970s.

Old Arabic print of team formations

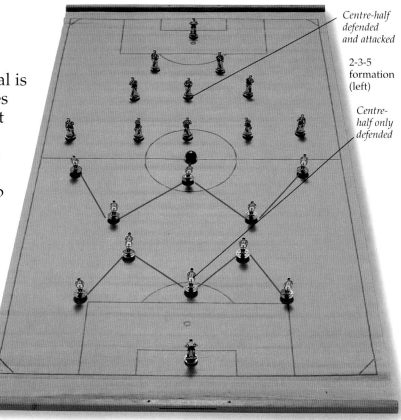

Centre-half defended and attacked

2-3-5 formation (left)

Centre-half only defended

W-M formation (right)

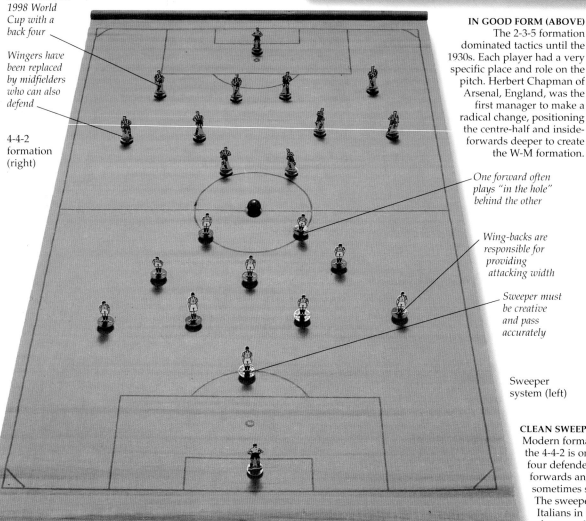

France won the 1998 World Cup with a back four

Wingers have been replaced by midfielders who can also defend

4-4-2 formation (right)

One forward often plays "in the hole" behind the other

Wing-backs are responsible for providing attacking width

Sweeper must be creative and pass accurately

Sweeper system (left)

IN GOOD FORM (ABOVE)
The 2-3-5 formation dominated tactics until the 1930s. Each player had a very specific place and role on the pitch. Herbert Chapman of Arsenal, England, was the first manager to make a radical change, positioning the centre-half and inside-forwards deeper to create the W-M formation.

GAME PLAN (ABOVE)
Managers use a board like this in the dressing room. They use it to show players how to counteract the opposition and where they should be at certain points in the game. This is particularly important when defending corners and free kicks.

CLEAN SWEEP
Modern formations are very varied, but the 4-4-2 is one of the most popular. The four defenders are not expected to push forwards and the four midfielders sometimes switch to a diamond shape. The sweeper system, perfected by the Italians in the 1960s, frees one player from marking duties to act as cover.

The forward cannot go "one on one" with the goalkeeper

OFFSIDE ORIGINS
The first offside law stated that three defenders, including the goalkeeper, had to be between the attacker and the goal when the ball was being played forwards by a team-mate. By 1920, fewer and fewer goals were being scored because, even if attackers were onside at the vital point, they still had to beat the last outfield defender.

OFFSIDE UPDATED
In 1925, FIFA decided to amend the offside law so that only two players had to be between the attacker and the goal. Immediately, far more goals were scored. The offside rule is basically unchanged today. Here, the midfielder is about to pass the ball to the forward. This player is still onside and, once in possession of the ball, will have only the goalkeeper to beat.

Player is offside

OFFSIDE TRAP
Teams without a sweeper, like Norway under Egil Olsen, are still able to use an offside trap. As the midfielder prepares to pass the ball forwards, the defenders suddenly advance up the field in a line, leaving the forward offside when the ball is played. William McCracken of Newcastle, England, was famous for first perfecting this tactic, in the years before the First World War.

PACKED DEFENCE
Denial of space to the opposition forwards is vital and certain players may be singled out for man-to-man marking. It is often said that the best teams are built from the back, with a strong defence providing a springboard for attack. Here, several defenders are surrounding a striker.

The attacker is trapped

The defenders are physically blocking the attacker in

NO SUBSTITUTE
Substitutions were first allowed by FIFA in 1923, but only if a player was injured. Injuries were faked so often to let coaches make tactical changes that it was gradually accepted that one player could be freely replaced. Now the number of substitutes allowed per team has increased to five for some games.

BE PREPARED
Javier Zanetti's goal for Argentina against England at France '98 was an example of how a well-rehearsed routine can work brilliantly. Lots of goals are scored from set-pieces – movements that a team practise before a match. Coaches spend a great deal of time going through these with the team in training.

Injury time

A PROFESSIONAL FOOTBALLER'S job involves far more than playing matches and enjoying the limelight. Training, fitness, and recovery from injuries are day-to-day concerns for the modern player. Advances in medicine mean that injuries that a few years ago would have led to inevitable retirement, can now be successfully treated. The pace of the modern game is unrelenting and loss of fitness is likely to stop a player from staying at the top level. Physiotherapy, nutrition, and even psychology are all parts of the conditioning programme of big clubs today.

Mr Black the footballer from a Happy Families game

FIGHTING FIT
Medicine balls like this were used in football training for many decades. They are extremely heavy, so throwing them improves stamina and also builds muscle bulk. Sophisticated gym equipment, training programmes, and resistance machines are now commonly used. Strength and fitness are essential to success in the modern game because top players have to play as many as 70 games per season. The greatest players are superb athletes as much as they are skilled footballers.

4 - CAMPIONATI MONDIALI DI CALCIO
NOVO: il brodo ricco di 12 saporiti ingredienti
Riproduzione vietata   Spiegazione a tergo

VITAL EDGE
Vittorio Pozzo, one of the first great managers, led Italy to victory in the World Cup in 1934 and 1938. He realized the importance of physical fitness and made his team train hard to give them a vital edge over their opponents. This paid off in extra time in the 1934 final, when Italy eventually scored the winning goal.

WARM UP AND COOL DOWN
A proper match-day routine can help to prolong a player's footballing career. Modern players are aware of the importance of warming-up thoroughly before a game. The risk of muscle tears and strains is significantly reduced if the muscles are warm and loose. Recovery after games is also important. Many teams "warm down" after a match to relax their muscles before resting them.

The stretcher is carried by two wooden poles

A pillow is built into the stretcher

A piece of canvas supports the injured player

GETTING CARRIED AWAY
This stretcher was used in the 1920s. In those days, if the stretcher was brought out on the pitch, the crowd knew that a player was seriously injured. Today, players are given a few moments to get up before they are carried off to prevent time-wasting and a delay to the game. They often run on again shortly afterwards. In the USA, motorized buggies or carts have taken the place of traditional stretchers.

AS IF BY MAGIC ...
The "magic" sponge has a special place in football folklore. Spectators have often wondered how a rub down with a sponge and cold water could result in a player's swift recovery from an injury. Today, the team physiotherapist, rather than the trainer, treats players for injury problems on the pitch and off it. Physiotherapists are fully qualified to give sophisticated treatment to injured players.

The sponge is still used in amateur games

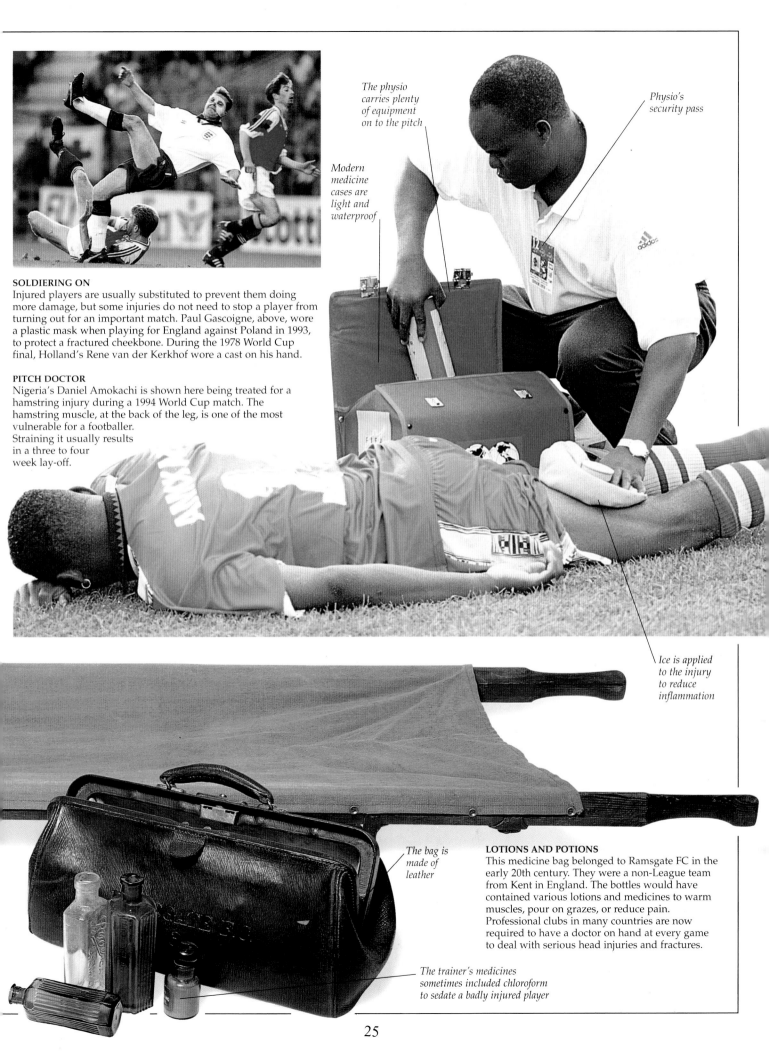

The physio carries plenty of equipment on to the pitch

Physio's security pass

Modern medicine cases are light and waterproof

SOLDIERING ON
Injured players are usually substituted to prevent them doing more damage, but some injuries do not need to stop a player from turning out for an important match. Paul Gascoigne, above, wore a plastic mask when playing for England against Poland in 1993, to protect a fractured cheekbone. During the 1978 World Cup final, Holland's Rene van der Kerkhof wore a cast on his hand.

PITCH DOCTOR
Nigeria's Daniel Amokachi is shown here being treated for a hamstring injury during a 1994 World Cup match. The hamstring muscle, at the back of the leg, is one of the most vulnerable for a footballer. Straining it usually results in a three to four week lay-off.

Ice is applied to the injury to reduce inflammation

The bag is made of leather

LOTIONS AND POTIONS
This medicine bag belonged to Ramsgate FC in the early 20th century. They were a non-League team from Kent in England. The bottles would have contained various lotions and medicines to warm muscles, pour on grazes, or reduce pain. Professional clubs in many countries are now required to have a doctor on hand at every game to deal with serious head injuries and fractures.

The trainer's medicines sometimes included chloroform to sedate a badly injured player

Footballs

An 1890s brass travelling inkwell in the shape of a football

Much of the appeal of football lies in the fact that it can be played without any special equipment. Children everywhere know that a tin can, some bound-up rags, or a ball from a different sport entirely, can be satisfyingly kicked around. This ingenuity was first displayed hundreds of years ago, when people discovered that an animal's bladder could be inflated and knotted to provide a light, bouncy ball. A bladder alone did not last very long so people began to protect the bladders in a shell made of animal skin cured to turn it into leather. This design worked so well that it is still used today but with modern, synthetic materials rather than animal products.

HEAVY GOING

Balls of the 1870s were often formed by stitching together eight segments of leather, the ends of which were secured by a central disc. They were heavy and it was impossible to kick them any great distance. Heading the ball could even prove fatal, especially if it was raining and the ball absorbed water. For obvious reasons, heading was not a technique often used in those days. The dribbling game was the popular style and the heavy ball was suitable for this style of play.

Manufacturers' names were first stencilled on balls in about 1900

The lace for tightening the case stands proud

Interlocking panels of leather

Sections of leather sewn together

Tool for lacing the ball tightly

Copper stencil

MADE TO MEASURE

This ball was used in March 1912, in the international match between Wales and England at Wrexham, Wales. England won the match 2–0. Made from a pig's bladder wrapped in cowhide, it is typical of the type of ball used for most of this century. The outside shell was laced up. The size and weight of footballs were standardized by 1912 but the balls still absorbed water and were prone to losing their shape.

The colours are based on the French flag

Brand name marked on the ball with a stencil

WORLD CUP COLOURS

The first World Cup balls to have a colour other than black were used in the Finals in France in 1998. They had a shiny, synthetic coating to make them waterproof and incorporated a layer of foam between the latex bladder and polyester skin. This let players pass and shoot quickly and also put spin and swerve on the ball. Like 75 percent of the world's footballs, they were made in the Sialkot region of Pakistan.

HEADING FOR TROUBLE

Balls like this were used in the 1966 World Cup Finals, at which time ball design had hardly changed in 50 years. The leather case was backed with a lining, a development of the 1940s that improved durability. The outside was painted with a pigment that helped to repel some water from a rain-soaked pitch. Manufacturers had still not found a reliable alternative to lacing up the ball so players risked injury when they headed the ball.

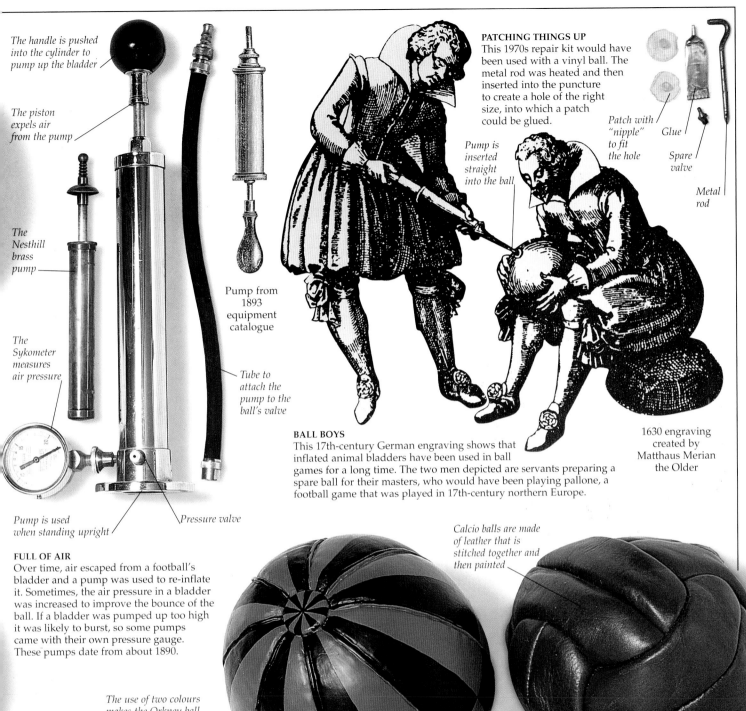

The handle is pushed into the cylinder to pump up the bladder

The piston expels air from the pump

The Nesthill brass pump

The Sykometer measures air pressure

Pump is used when standing upright

Pressure valve

Pump from 1893 equipment catalogue

Tube to attach the pump to the ball's valve

PATCHING THINGS UP
This 1970s repair kit would have been used with a vinyl ball. The metal rod was heated and then inserted into the puncture to create a hole of the right size, into which a patch could be glued.

Pump is inserted straight into the ball

Patch with "nipple" to fit the hole

Glue

Spare valve

Metal rod

BALL BOYS
This 17th-century German engraving shows that inflated animal bladders have been used in ball games for a long time. The two men depicted are servants preparing a spare ball for their masters, who would have been playing pallone, a football game that was played in 17th-century northern Europe.

1630 engraving created by Matthaus Merian the Older

FULL OF AIR
Over time, air escaped from a football's bladder and a pump was used to re-inflate it. Sometimes, the air pressure in a bladder was increased to improve the bounce of the ball. If a bladder was pumped up too high it was likely to burst, so some pumps came with their own pressure gauge. These pumps date from about 1890.

Calcio balls are made of leather that is stitched together and then painted

The use of two colours makes the Orkney ball flash in the air

Alternative balls
Several different football games are played around the world today. They each use a ball particular to that game. Some football games have existed for centuries. The balls may have features connected to a ceremonial aspect of the game, and involve decoration and colour, or they may be designed to withstand harsh treatment. In some modern games the ball has evolved along with the game.

SHAPING UP
The game of American football was originally based on kicking a ball. As throwing became a central feature, the present shape of the ball evolved. The small ball can be gripped firmly, making it easier for the quarterback to make long, accurate passes.

OFFICIAL 191 Cooper

BUILT TO LAST
In the Scottish Orkney Isles, a type of football game is played through the streets every New Year. The ball is much heavier than a normal football and is stuffed tightly with pieces of cork. This helps it to last for several hours of play and also makes it float on water – a useful feature because a team can score a goal by throwing the ball into the sea.

MADE TO MATCH
Calcio, first played in Italy in the 16th century, was re-introduced to Florence in 1930. The game is played by teams of 27 a side, all wearing medieval clothes and armour. Balls of various colours are used including green, white, and red to match the costumes. Calcio balls are smaller than regular footballs, making it easier for the players to pick them up and throw them.

Football boots

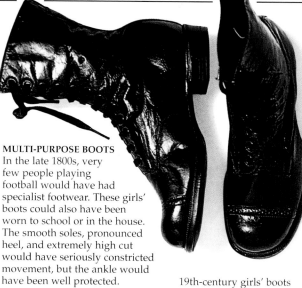

OF ALL FOOTBALL equipment, boots have changed most over the last 100 years. Always the most expensive item of kit, they remain an unaffordable luxury to many players around the world who have to play in bare feet. The fast, agile sport we see today would simply not be possible if football players had to use the heavy, cumbersome boots worn up until the 1930s. Professionals then dreaded having to "break in" hard, new boots, which involved a great deal of pain. They preferred to patch up an old pair again and again until they fell apart. In the first World Cup tournaments in the 1930s, the South American teams wore lighter, low cut boots, much to the astonishment of the Europeans. These began the trend towards the modern, high-tech boot.

A 1950s painting of football boots called *Christopher's Boots*, by Doris Brand

MULTI-PURPOSE BOOTS
In the late 1800s, very few people playing football would have had specialist footwear. These girls' boots could also have been worn to school or in the house. The smooth soles, pronounced heel, and extremely high cut would have seriously constricted movement, but the ankle would have been well protected.

19th-century girls' boots

1920s child's boots

A "kick around" is a popular pastime with children

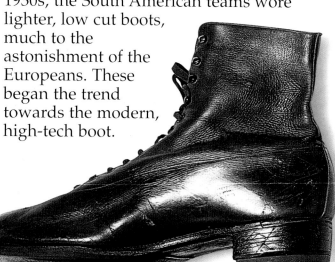

MADE FOR THE JOB
By the 1920s, football boots, like the "Manfield Hotspur" were being mass-produced for footballers of all ages. Children's boots were designed just like adults', with reinforced toe-caps and heels, some ankle protection, and leather studs. Social conditions at the time, though, meant that most working-class families could not afford such equipment and, if they could, they would have handed down boots from one child to another.

Extra foot support

Cotton laces

STUDLESS BOOTS
A 19th-century gentleman footballer wore studless boots, which would not have allowed for sharp turns or long passing. However, they were practical enough for the type of dribbling game favoured by the great English amateur teams like the Corinthians. This style of play was dictated by the confined spaces used for football practice at many British public schools. Boots like these would have doubled in weight when wet.

BOOTS IN THE BATH
In 1910 these boots were marketed as "Cup Final Specials", an early example of a football product being tied to a famous match. The wickerwork pattern on the toes was one of several designs that were thought to help a player control the ball – a major part of modern boot design too. It was common for a player to wear a new pair of boots in the bath for a few hours to soften the leather.

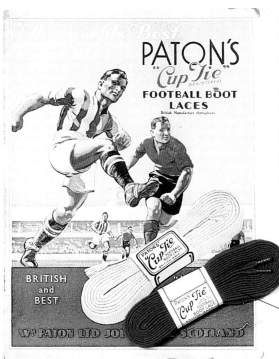

LOTS OF LACES
Paton's bootlaces, in various colours, were widely used from the 1930s onwards. There was a constant demand for replacements because repeated soaking during matches, followed by drying out, caused the early cotton laces to perish and eventually snap.

PERSONALIZED BOOTS
Boots of a colour other than black or brown are a feature of the modern game. Moustafa Hadji of Morocco was one of several players to wear a different colour at the 1998 World Cup. However, they were not unknown in the past. Puma produced a white boot in 1958, and England player Alan Ball was known for his white boots a decade later.

Flexible ankle support

Laces were wrapped around the boots for a closer fit

England's Tom Finney promoted these boots

White laces were common in the 1930s

THE MODERN LOOK
The classic black-with-white-trim design, which is still used today, began to be popular in the 1950s. The vertical strap on the instep remains from earlier designs. The boots were becoming flexible enough to be worn without much breaking-in. There was less protection around the ankle, which allowed players more freedom of movement but led to an increase in injuries. It was at this time that boot-makers began to use the name of famous players to sell their boots.

THE DESIGNER AGE
A vast amount of money is spent on the research and development of modern boots. Top-quality leather uppers, usually made from kangaroo hides, and light, synthetic soles combine to make boots that last. They are comfortable and allow the best players to put amazing amounts of spin on the ball. Competition among manufacturers is intense and huge amounts of money are spent on advertizing.

Studs are screwed into the sole

Studs and stuff
The number of studs on the sole, and the way in which they are positioned, varies greatly. Longer studs are needed if the pitch is wet and muddy, shorter ones are worn if the pitch is hard. The potential they have to cause injury has always been a concern to the game's governing bodies – in the 1930s, the wearing of illegal boots was a sending-off offence. Since 1900, one of the jobs of the referee or an assistant has been to check the studs of every player entering the field of play. Anybody wearing boots with sharp edges or protruding nails is not allowed to play.

Wooden hammer

Nails fixed to studs

Separate nails

Key for tightening the studs

THE FIRST STUDS
Early football boots were made entirely of leather. The studs had to be hammered into the soles.

HARMFUL HAMMERS
Rubber studs came next. They also needed nailing to the sole and it was not long before the boots were damaged.

ALL CHANGE!
Modern screw-in studs are made of plastic or metal. Players can change their studs at half-time, to adjust to changes in conditions.

Football outfits

Shirts, shorts, and socks were described as the basis of a footballer's outfit in the first Laws of 1863 and they remain so today. The materials used for a footballer's outfit have changed since then. Players in South America and Mediterranean countries needed clothing suitable for warm climates, so wool gave way to cotton and then artificial fibres. Cool fabrics that "breathe" are now the norm worldwide. Teams wear matching outfits, or strips, on the field of play. The colours are the colours of the club, with which all the fans can identify. Most clubs and international sides have a home and an away strip in case two teams wear the same colours.

In the 19th century, both football and rugby players wore knee-length knickerbockers with no leg protection.

DUTCH ORANGE
The Holland strip is unusual in being orange, and is recognized all around the world. The Dutch fans wear replica shirts and other orange clothes to form a mass of colour at matches. Here, Marc Overmars is on the ball for Holland during the 1998 World Cup Finals.

WOOLLY JUMPERS
In the late 19th century, football jerseys were often made from wool. They tended to stretch out of shape and could become heavy in the rain because they soaked up water.

AWAY STRIP
In the 1966 World Cup final, the England team wore light cotton shirts with a round collar. Although England were playing at home, they did not wear their normal white home strip because West Germany were wearing white. They wore red instead.

LACE-UPS
At all levels of the game, teams began to wear matching strips. This black-and-white shirt was worn by a member of Newcastle United's team for the 1908 English FA Cup final. Newcastle still wear black-and-white today. The shirt is made of thick cotton with a lace-up collar. Lace-up collars became fashionable again in the 1990s and were worn by Manchester United, among other teams.

AUSTRALIAN AMATEURS
This Australian shirt is made from wool with a cotton collar. It was worn in 1925 by the player Tommy Traynor. Shirts worn in international matches have symbolic importance. At the end of the game, the teams swap shirts with each other in a gesture of goodwill.

KEEPING COOL
Today, most shirts are designed to keep players cool and draw away excess moisture. This 1994 Brazil World Cup shirt is made of light, synthetic fabrics. With the energetic pace of modern games, such improvements are vital, especially for matches played in hot climates.

FAIR-WEATHER FRIENDS
By the early-20th century, manufacturers in many countries had begun to adapt the kit that British players had taken overseas with them in the 19th century. They produced lighter outfits more suited to warm climates. Short-sleeved shirts and deep V-neck collars became part of the typical Mediterranean look, as represented on this image from Valencia in Spain.

Early 1900s Spanish illustration

These socks are unusually decorative

Women were not expected to head the ball

PULL YOUR SOCKS UP
These socks from the 1920s look just the same as modern ones but they are made of wool. Modern socks are made of synthetic materials, making them more comfortable. Players keep up their socks with ties around the top. The ties can be made from strips of bandage or elasticated tape cut up into lengths. Towards the end of a gruelling match, when players are prone to cramp, they may discard the tie-ups. Socks around the ankle can be a tell-tale sign of a tired footballer facing defeat.

High kicking was easier if shorts were above the knees

Hoops and stripes are classic design features

Cream flannel shorts from about 1900

Modern synthetic shorts with decorative side seams

Hard-wearing cotton shorts from the 1930s

Early 20th-century French illustration

UNDER WRAPS
Until the First World War, women footballers had to keep their hair under a cap or bonnet and hide their legs inside voluminous bloomers. In the 1910s, when many men were away at war, crowds flocked to see women's exhibition matches. This wider acceptance of ladies' football enabled women's teams to start wearing football outfits that were similar to those worn by men and more suitable for the game.

SHORT STORY
Gentlemen amateurs in the 1860s played in full-length trousers but, as the game developed, players had to increase their speed and agility. Shorter knickerbockers cut just above the knee then became popular. The baggy style of football shorts of the 1930s was made famous by Alex James of Arsenal, England, "the wee man in the big shorts". This fashion was revived in the 1990s following a trend in the 1970s for tight shorts.

Accessories

INJURY AND DISCOMFORT were part of the game of football in its early days. When protective equipment and other accessories, such as hats, ear-muffs, and belts, were introduced at the end of the 19th century, they helped to distance the game from its rather violent past. Shin-pads were developed in 1874 by Samuel Widdowson in response to the physical punishment that players suffered during games. Leg protection is still part of kit today, but other accessories are no longer used.

Catalogue illustration of protective ear-muffs

Buttoned tunic was an alternative to the more common shirt

Leather buckles fasten these shin-pads

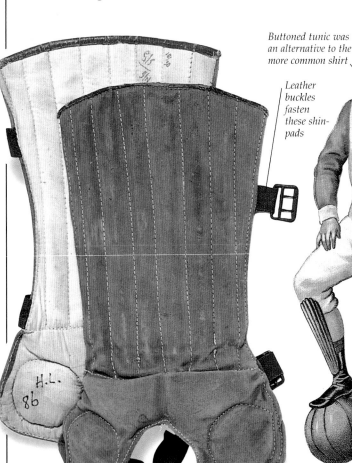

LASTING DESIGN
In the 1900s, players would have worn shin-pads like these outside their socks, held in place with straps and buckles. The front section is made of leather and the back of cotton, with a stuffing in between of animal hair. This mix of materials was used in shin-pads until the 1960s.

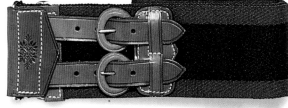

RE-INFORCED GUARDS
This figure is from a picture on the box of an early 20th-century German football game. His shin-pads, worn over the top of his socks and knickerbockers, appear to be strengthened with cane bars.

BELT UP
Decorative belts were a part of many schoolboys' football kits until the 20th century. They smartened up appearances by holding in the shirt and gave teams identity through the use of colours. Belts were also part of women's kit in the early 1900s.

Early 20th-century schoolboys' belts

Woman's belt from 1895

THE FIRST SHIN-PADS
The earliest shin-pads were worn outside the socks and were extended to include ankle protectors, which rested on the top of the boot. Some, like these, had a suede covering, which was more prone to water damage than other types of leather. These heavy and inflexible pads date from the 1890s, about 20 years after shin-pads became part of the footballer's kit.

1980s shin-pads were similar in shape to those from the 1930s

Long laces to wrap around the leg twice

ROOM TO MOVE
By 1910, ankle protection was no longer part of shin-pad design, not because it was not needed, but because it restricted movement of the foot. Passing and running off the ball had become important parts of the game, requiring increased flexibility of the ankle. Players were therefore forced to sacrifice some protection. Cork was sometimes used to strengthen pads.

TIE-ON SHIN-PADS
Shin-pads worn inside the socks had taken over by 1930. Laces were used for fastening instead of buckles, to prevent chafing on the players' legs. Many years later, tighter-fitting synthetic, rather than woollen, socks held the pads firmly in position without the need for ties of any sort.

LIGHTWEIGHT PROTECTION
Modern shin-pads look dramatically different from earlier models. They are shaped to fit the leg, using lightweight materials to give excellent protection. Even the delicate Achilles tendon at the back of the ankle is shielded. The revival of ankle protectors, after a gap of 100 years, brings shin-pad design full circle.

KEEPING WARM
Gloves have become common, especially among players from hot countries, such as Brazil, who play in Europe, often in freezing temperatures. Players susceptible to hamstring and groin injuries are encouraged to wear undershorts because they help to keep these important muscles warm.

Ladies wore hats to keep long hair out of the mud

Stripes to match team colours

Women's football hats

FOOTBALL FIGURE
This porcelain figure of a boy was made in Germany in the 1890s. Artistic depictions of football from this period often showed players wearing hats, even though they were becoming decorative rather than practical items.

Hand-painted German figure

Brazilian footballer Emerson

HATS OFF!
These women's hats date from 1895, when ladies' football was still in its infancy. The fact that women played in hats does not mean that theirs was a gentler game. Like the men, many female players wore shin-pads for protection.

Famous players

Football is a team game. Clubs and national sides inspire the greatest passion among fans but a few players are so gifted and entertaining that they stand out from their team-mates and draw thousands of extra people to matches. Some great players are famous for their spirit of fair play, while others have been surrounded by controversy and bad publicity. But all of the great players share an ability to change the course of a match through a moment of incredible individual skill.

GORDON BANKS (b. 1937)
English goalkeeper Gordon Banks is remembered for one save in particular – a spectacular effort that kept out Pele's header in the 1970 World Cup. Banks won 73 caps between 1963 and 1972 and would have won more, but for an eye injury.

JOHANN CRUYFF (b. 1947)
One of the few great players also to have become a successful manager, Cruyff was able to instill in his teams some of the style and tactical awareness that made him such a joy to watch. He played for Holland, Ajax, and Barcelona, Spain. He personified the concept of "total football" by floating all over the pitch and using his amazing balance and skill to open up defences.

GERD MULLER (b. 1945)
Known as *"Der Bomber"*, Gerd Muller was an unlikely looking centre-forward. He had an astonishing spring in his heels, which made up for his lack of height. He was a prolific goal scorer, with 68 goals in 62 games for West Germany. Most of his club football was played with Bayern Munich, Germany, for whom he scored a record 365 goals.

Milla was a great entertainer, known for his flamboyant goal celebrations

Roger Milla after scoring for Cameroon against Colombia in the 1990 World Cup

ROGER MILLA (b. 1952)
Twice African player of the year, Roger Milla of Cameroon was the first player to become famous worldwide playing for an African country. He was also the oldest player to appear and score in a World Cup Finals in 1994, aged 42.

BOBBY CHARLTON (b. 1937)
Manchester United star, Bobby Charlton survived the Munich air crash that killed seven of his team-mates in 1958. Known for the power and accuracy of his shooting, he was invaluable in England's 1966 World Cup win. He was knighted in 1994.

Eusebio practises ball control in training

Eusebio scored 38 goals in 46 internationals

DIEGO MARADONA (b. 1960)
Maradona was the best player of his generation and also one of the most controversial. He had a tremendous ability to inspire his team-mates, most notably when leading Argentina to the 1986 World Cup and Napoli to two Serie A titles in Italy in the late 1980s. His magical left foot and strength in possession were his main assets.

Maradona's low centre of gravity gave him excellent balance

In the 1986 World Cup against England, Maradona scored two goals – one a handball that should have been disallowed, the other a dazzling solo effort

EUSEBIO (b. 1942)
Although he was born in Mozambique, Eusebio was snapped up by Benfica of Lisbon, Portugal, and went on to play for Portugal, in common with several other talented players. He starred in the 1962 European Cup final, scoring twice as Benfica beat Real Madrid, Spain, 5–3. Eusebio was respected all over the world for his fair play and dignity as well as for his footballing talent.

Meazza (below right) shakes hands with Hungarian captain, Sarosi, before the 1938 World Cup final

Like many of the greatest players, Maradona liked to be number 10

GARRINCHA (b. 1933)
Nicknamed "the Little Bird", Garrincha had polio as a child. He overcame his disability to become one of the quickest and most elusive wingers the game has seen. He played on the right-hand side of Brazil's legendary 1958 forward line. In 1962, he made up for the absence of the injured Pele with some brilliant performances, helping Brazil to retain the World Cup.

GUISEPPE MEAZZA (b. 1910)
Italian Giuseppe Meazza won two World Cup winner's medals in 1934 and 1938. He was respected as a creator and scorer of goals from his inside-forward position. In 1938, he organized the Italian team when the coach, Pozzo, was ordered to leave the bench and sit in the stands. He spent his best years at Internazionale of Milan, Italy, and won 53 caps.

Maradona's magical footwork entertained and amazed the fans

COUPE DU MONDE 1938

35

Continued on next page

MARCO VAN BASTEN (b. 1964)
Van Basten of Holland scored one of the greatest goals of all time at the European Championship final in 1988 – a volley from wide of the goal. Sadly, an ankle injury cut short his career.

LUIS SUAREZ (B. 1935)
Considered one of the best-ever Spanish footballers, Luis Suarez dominated the midfield for Barcelona, Spain, in the late 1950s. By the mid-1960s, he was playing a key part in Italian Inter Milan's new *catenaccio* system – a line-up heavy on defence with only two forward players. He was famous for his fast breaks out of defence and accurate passes. Suarez went on to be manager of Spain at the 1990 World Cup.

Kopa was the greatest French player of the 1950s

Kopa was known for his careful ball control and well-thought-out passing

Van Basten was the best centre-forward of the late 1980s

RAYMOND KOPA (b. 1931)
Creative midfielder Raymond Kopa made his name with French club, Reims. He led them to the first European Cup final in 1956, where they lost to Spain's Real Madrid. Kopa played for France at the 1958 World Cup and was named European Footballer of the Year in 1959.

The two defenders are playing for the Italian club Roma

Roma defenders are left in Platini's wake

STANLEY MATTHEWS (b. 1915)
England's Stanley Matthews was known for his dribbling skills. One of his finest performances was in Blackpool's 4–3 win over Bolton in the 1953 English FA Cup final. He won 84 caps and was still playing football for Stoke City at the age of 50. He was knighted in 1965.

LEV YASHIN (b. 1929)
Always kitted out in black, Lev Yashin was rivalled only by Gordon Banks as the greatest goalkeeper of his era. He played for the Soviet Union in three World Cups and is, to this day, the only goalkeeper to have been named European Footballer of the Year.

Between them, Puskas and Di Stefano scored seven goals in the European Cup final in 1960

FRANZ BECKENBAUER (b. 1945)

Beckenbauer's intelligence shone out on the field as he dictated play from a deep sweeper position. Together with Johann Cruyff, he is one of the few football-playing legends to achieve similar success as a manager. Having captained West Germany at the 1974 World Cup, he managed them when they won again in 1990.

FERENC PUSKAS (b. 1927)

The star of Hungary's famous team of the 1950s, Ferenc Puskas was part of the Hungarian team that beat England 6–3 at Wembley in 1953. He joined Real Madrid of Spain in 1958. Puskas strongly favoured his left foot, scoring a wealth of stunning goals for both club and country.

ALFREDO DI STEFANO (b. 1926)

When Real Madrid dominated European football in the 1950s, Di Stefano was one of their star players. His stamina enabled him to contribute all over the field. He and Puskas formed one of football's legendary double acts.

MICHEL PLATINI (b. 1955)

Platini was one of those players who seemed happy to take the weight of a nation's expectations on his shoulders. He captained France in the 1984 European Championships, and they won the tournament for the first time. Platini was an attacking midfielder who often finished as top scorer at Italian club Juventus.

Michel Platini playing for Juventus

Platini had the speed and foresight to move forwards into space

PELE (b. 1940)

Many people's choice of the greatest player of all, Pele was king of Brazilian football from the late 1950s to early 1970s. He overcame constant fouling by frustrated defenders to score more than 1,000 goals for Brazilian club Santos, American soccer team New York Cosmos, and the Brazilian national team. His enthusiasm and obvious love of playing, despite being plagued by injury, make him a perfect role model for the game of football.

Medals and caps

Sew-on badge given to members of an international squad

IT IS THE AIM OF ALL footballers to play well and win each game. Those lucky enough to win a championship are awarded a medal as a mark of their achievement. Those good enough to be picked to play for their country win a cap. Medals and caps have been part of the game since the 19th century and are still highly valued rewards today. At the highest level, success can be measured by the number of caps a player has and passing the "100 cap" mark is considered exceptional service to the national team. Thomas Ravelli of Sweden won 138 caps – a record for a European.

Argentine pot made from a dried aubergine trimmed with silver

Ornate silver dagger

Norwegian silver spoon

Argentine silver spoon

Medals

As with military medals for soldiers, footballers are rewarded with medals for helping their side, not for a moment of personal glory. Medals are awarded at all levels of football, professional and amateur. They are mementoes by which players can remember their glory days and can become valuable collectors' items.

GOOD SPORT
Before organized leagues were established, football medals were often awarded for sportsmanship as well as victories. The full-back C Duckworth was given this medal for "gentlemanly and successful play" in the 1883–84 season.

WITH COMPLIMENTS
This "complimentary medal for defeating all comers" was awarded in the 1884–85 season.

PRECIOUS GIFTS
As well as caps and medals, international players are sometimes presented with gifts by opposing football associations. The England team each received a silver spoon when they faced Norway in 1949. The Argentine FA gave the English team members ceremonial daggers and other silver items on their first visit to Wembley, England, in 1951.

English v Scottish League 1893

FA Cup runners-up 1893

Lancashire Cup winners 1887

DOUBLE
This group of medals belonged to R H Howarth of the Preston North End "Invincibles". The team won the League and the FA Cup in 1888–89, achieving the first English "double".

TROPHY TRIUMPH
This plaque was made to commemorate an international match between France and England in 1947. All the English players received a plaque after winning the match 3–0.

CLUB STRIKERS
Some clubs strike their own medals to mark a special achievement of their players. This medal was awarded at the end of a season to players of a team that had won their league.

1909 Hungarian medal

PLAY-OFF PRIZES
Medals have been presented to the winners of the third and fourth place play-off match at every World Cup Finals, except 1930 and 1950. At France '98, Croatia won third place medals, defeating Holland 2–1 with goals from Robert Prosinecki and Davor Suker.

HUNGARY FOR SUCCESS
Hungary was one of the first European countries to take to football. They copied the way other countries organized the game, including the awarding of medals. This medal was awarded to the members of an international side after a match against Austria in 1909.

CHAMPIONS
This medal was awarded to a player for success in the 1914–15 season.

AMATEUR
This 1920s medal was given to a successful amateur player.

ARSENAL STAR
This 1930s medal may have belonged to football star Alex James.

Caps

A coloured cap was once the only way of showing to which side a player belonged. Then, in 1872, the FA ruled that teams should wear distinctive shirts. In 1886, it was suggested that caps be awarded to footballers each time they played for their country. Today, they are given to every member of a national team, including substitutes. Often, only one cap is awarded for a series of games so a player with 50 "caps" has fewer actual ones.

HOME CAP
This Welsh cap was awarded for the 1903–04 Home International matches between England, Scotland, Northern Ireland, and Wales. This tournament took place every year until 1984.

CAREY'S CAP
The great defender Johnny Carey won this cap when he played for Ireland against Poland and Switzerland in 1938. Carey won 36 caps.

Tassels are added for decoration

Welsh national crest – a dragon

Details of matches can be embroidered into each panel

The date covers games from a whole season

Football caps are usually made from velvet

Northern Ireland had its own team from 1921

SCHOOL COLOURS
Football caps were first awarded in English public schools. "Colours", in the form of caps, were given to the most able players in each year.

IN TRAINING
It is not only players that are rewarded for their efforts. Trainer Will Scott received this medal when the English and Scottish Leagues met at Celtic Park, Glasgow, Scotland in November 1931.

WAR GAMES
Throughout the Second World War, famous international players took part in exhibition matches arranged to boost public morale. In 1946, Tom Finney was given this set of three medals after appearing in a match in Antwerp, Belgium.

PROMOTIONAL MEDAL
By the 1950s, businesses had started to commemorate a range of football events. The French newspaper, *Le Soir*, made this medal to mark a club tour of Austria in 1953.

WORLD CUP
The biggest football achievement is victory in the World Cup final. This is a replica of the Jules Rimet medal given to West Germany's winning players in 1954.

AFRICAN CUP
This medal was presented to the winners of the first African Nations' Cup in 1957. The competition was held in Khartoum, Sudan, and only Sudan, Ethiopia, and Egypt took part. Egypt beat Ethiopia 4–0 in the final.

Famous clubs

CLUBS INSPIRE the greatest loyalty and passion from football fans, more so even than national teams. In every country, certain big clubs attract followers from beyond their local areas and tend to dominate their domestic leagues and cups. Success for these clubs often continues because financial backing ensures a steady supply of good new players. In all corners of the world, people swear allegiance to Barcelona or Liverpool, Flamengo or Milan, although they may never be able to attend a game involving their team.

BRAVO BENFICA
Only Porto and Sporting Lisbon rival Benfica in the Portuguese League. Benfica have also had some notable victories on the more competitive European stage. Benfica were the great team of the early 1960s, winning two European Cups, in 1961 and 1962, and reaching but losing three further finals.

This bronze depicts Benfica's symbol, an eagle

Figure of the ancient Greek hero Ajax forms the basis of the Dutch club's crest

The club Ajax was formed in Amsterdam in 1900

MIGHTY MARSEILLE
In 1993, Marseille, led by the attacking threat of Allen Boksic and Rudi Voller, beat AC Milan of Italy 1–0 to lift the European Cup. French administrators, such as long-time FIFA President Jules Rimet, have always had a large role in football but it was 1993 before a French team won a European trophy.

LONDON LADIES
Netty Honeyball was the force behind the first great women's team in the 1890s. The British Ladies Club drew large crowds for their exhibition matches in London at a time when the capital was lagging behind the North and Midlands of England with regard to football.

YOUNG TALENT
In the 1970s, Dutch club Ajax's policy to develop their own young players bore fruit. The players, including the star Johann Cruyff, helped Ajax to three consecutive European Cup wins in the 1970s and some of them helped the national team in two World Cups. Despite regularly selling their best players, the club returned to the forefront of European football in the mid 1990s.

BUSBY BABES
English club Manchester United started life as Newton Heath. They changed their name in 1902. The Munich air disaster of 1958, in which eight of manager Matt Busby's young team died, inspired sympathy around the world. Since then, the club have won two European Cups – in 1968 and 1999.

Baines card from the 1890s shows full-back, Jack Powell.

PLAY UP NEWTON HEATH

POWELL

THE GOLDEN YEARS
Bayern Munich followed Ajax as the leading European team in the early 1970s. They won three consecutive European Cups with the help of players such as Franz Beckenbauer, Gerd Muller, and Sepp Maier, who were also important to the German national team.

Paul Breitner of Bayern Munich in 1974

Dominguez, the goalkeeper – from Argentina

Alfredo di Stefano, the leader of the team

Francisco Gento, the fast left winger

REAL RIVALRY
In the late 1950s, Real Madrid, Spain, possibly had the greatest club side ever. Legends such as Di Stefano and Puskas inspired this Spanish team to win the first five European Cups. Real Madrid have a spectacular stadium – the Bernabeu – and a bitter rivalry with Barcelona.

THE RED DEVILS
This picture shows the players Cagna and Rios of Independiente, Argentina, in 1995. In 1964, Independiente was the first Argentine club to win the South American club competition, the Copa Libertadores. The "Red Devils" went on to win the competition four more times between 1972 and 1975.

The fans

FOR ALL THE talent displayed by the players on the pitch, it is the fans who have made football the biggest game in the world. From the last years of the 19th century, working people began to have enough free time to attend sporting fixtures. They created an atmosphere of excitement and expectation, and large crowds became an important part of a match. Today, football is the most widely watched sport in the world. Fans are keener than ever to show their support for club and country in a range of noisy and colourful ways.

GONE BANANAS
In England in the late 1980s, there was a craze for taking large inflatables to matches. Fans waved bananas, fish, and fried eggs in the crowd to show their support for their teams.

PRESTON. N.E

Preston North End, England, rosette

Manchester City, England, pennant

Holland scarf

Lazio, Italy, scarf

CLUB COLOURS
Colours are a vital part of the bond between a team and its supporters. Once, people made rosettes for big matches and displayed pennants. Now, fans often wear a scarf to show their loyalty.

PERFECT VIEW
In their desperation to see a game, fans are not always put off by the "ground full" signs. In the 19th century, before large-scale stands were built, trees provided a convenient spot from which to watch a popular match.

RARE COLLECTION
Fans have always collected objects bearing images of football. Today, the items probably feature their favourite club but, in the past, designs were based on more general football scenes. Collecting autographs is also a popular hobby and offers a rare opportunity to meet star players.

Child's money-box

Jack Rowley, forward

John Aston, full-back

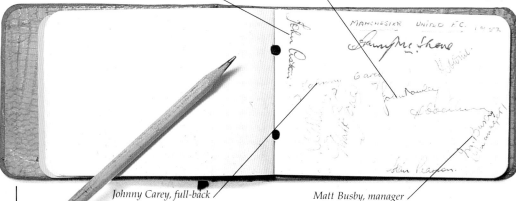

Johnny Carey, full-back

Matt Busby, manager

1950s autograph book containing signatures of famous figures of Manchester United, England

Wooden pencil case

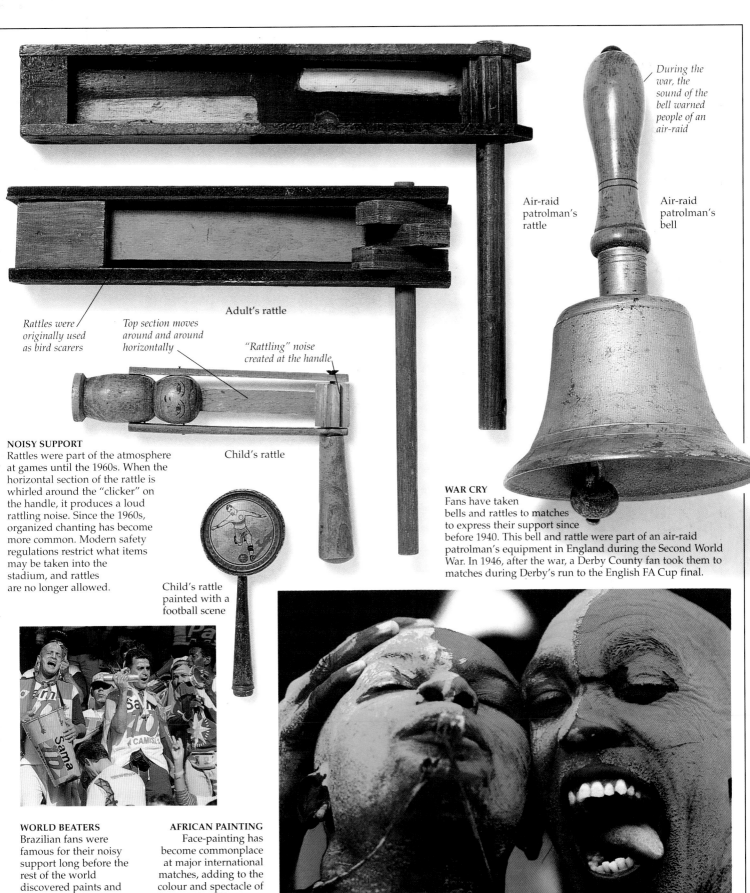

During the war, the sound of the bell warned people of an air-raid

Air-raid patrolman's rattle

Air-raid patrolman's bell

Adult's rattle

Rattles were originally used as bird scarers

Top section moves around and around horizontally

"Rattling" noise created at the handle

Child's rattle

NOISY SUPPORT
Rattles were part of the atmosphere at games until the 1960s. When the horizontal section of the rattle is whirled around the "clicker" on the handle, it produces a loud rattling noise. Since the 1960s, organized chanting has become more common. Modern safety regulations restrict what items may be taken into the stadium, and rattles are no longer allowed.

Child's rattle painted with a football scene

WAR CRY
Fans have taken bells and rattles to matches to express their support since before 1940. This bell and rattle were part of an air-raid patrolman's equipment in England during the Second World War. In 1946, after the war, a Derby County fan took them to matches during Derby's run to the English FA Cup final.

WORLD BEATERS
Brazilian fans were famous for their noisy support long before the rest of the world discovered paints and drums. They produce a samba beat on their drums and blow their whistles. As the noise echoes around the stands, the fans dance to accompany the action, especially if their team is winning.

AFRICAN PAINTING
Face-painting has become commonplace at major international matches, adding to the colour and spectacle of the occasion. Here, two Zambian fans, painted to reflect the team's colours, enjoy an African Nations Cup match. Face-painting is particularly popular with Dutch, Danish, and Japanese fans.

Match day

This is a scoreboard from an early 20th-century French football game.

THE ATMOSPHERE of a big game, the sound of the crowd, and the closeness of the players combine to make going to a live football match quite addictive. Even though football is now widely shown on television, millions of fans still go to the match. Many supporters, like players, are extremely superstitious and follow the same routine every time they go to a match. The crowd and the noisy support they give their team are essential to the game of football. It is vital that clubs continue to improve comfort and safety for their fans, so that they keep on coming back.

ALL DRESSED UP
This photo shows fans of West Ham, England, preparing to travel to the 1923 FA Cup final, the first to be held at Wembley. Many more than the official attendance of 123,000 crammed into the stadium. Notice the smart appearance of the supporters.

In the 1988 European Championship final, Holland beat the Soviet Union 2-0

Holograms and complicated designs are now used to deter ticket forgeries

TICKETS PLEASE
Tickets are essential in controlling access to games and keeping attendance to a safe level. Years ago, this was only necessary at cup finals and World Cup matches. Tickets were issued for general areas in the stadium. Now that terraces are being phased out in favour of seating, each match ticket corresponds to a particular seat.

READING MATTER
The earliest programmes were simple one-sheet items, giving only team line-ups. As football became more popular, further elements were added, such as a message from the manager and background information on the opposition. Glossy, full-colour brochures, largely paid for by advertising, are produced for tournaments such as the European Championships.

LET ME ENTERTAIN YOU
To make going to a match even more enjoyable, particularly for a family audience, clubs and governing bodies lay on extra entertainment before kick-off and at half-time. In the past, this may have taken the form of a brass band, but modern crowds expect something more elaborate. The opening ceremony at France '98 featured giant inflatable footballs.

A FAMILY AFFAIR
In the USA, a trip to a sporting event is usually a family day out, and the stadiums have good facilities for everybody. There is a lot of razzmatazz at the Major League Soccer matches. Cheerleaders and music keep the crowds well entertained. This is match day at the Kansas City Wizards' stadium.

1903 FA official's badge

Official badge from 1905

The badges are made of cloth and decorated with gold brocade

FA badge from 1898

The English three lions motif

ACCESS ALL AREAS?
Away from the mass of spectators, there are certain areas of the stadium, such as the boardroom, where access is strictly controlled. These badges, from 1898–1905, would have been sewn on blazers and worn by Football Association officials. These days, executive boxes have become a feature of many grounds.

Badge worn at 1899 England v Scotland international

CROWD CONTROL
Police and stewards attend football matches to ensure the safety of everybody at the game. Police, like these Italian officers at a Juventus match, may need to take a hard line with unruly fans, and sometimes use horses or dogs to help them control large crowds. They may also control traffic and escort supporters to and from the match.

COMING HOME
This drawing comes from a postcard from the early 20th century. The caption on the card says, "Our team's lost by ..... goals to ..... ". Space is left on the card for fans to fill in the score. Somehow, the depression of defeat is always replaced by excitement and high hopes when the next game comes around.

The stadium

SHEFFIELD WEDNESDAY F.C.

As CROWDS GREW EVER larger in the late 19th century, football clubs realized that they would have to build somewhere permanent to hold their matches. Stadiums became a necessity. They provided fans with shelter and a decent view of the game. They also created an atmosphere that added greatly to the match day experience. A series of stadium disasters over the years, in places such as Scotland, Peru, and Russia, finally led to widespread belief that the terraces should be replaced by all-seater stands for the safety of spectators.

TWIN TOWERS
The famous Twin Towers at Wembley Stadium in England will not be part of the new stadium being built for the 21st century.

THEN THERE WAS LIGHT...
Floodlights were first used in 1878 but they did not become standard at professional clubs until the 1950s. The most common form of stadium lighting was on tall pylons in the corners of the stadium. Today, lights are often placed in rows along the stand roof.

CROWD SAFETY
On 15 April 1989, the FA Cup semi-final at Hillsborough, Sheffield, was the scene of the worst disaster in English football history. More than 90 Liverpool fans died in a devastating crowd crush. The resulting report began a major leap forward in stadium safety – to prevent a similar disaster from ever happening again.

WORLD CUP WONDER
The Maracana Stadium in Rio de Janeiro, Brazil, is named after a river that runs nearby. It was built for the 1950 World Cup. It is a huge concrete oval and has remained a source of wonder despite problems with its decaying structure. All the clubs in Rio de Janeiro have their own grounds but use the Maracana for big matches. With its 120,000 capacity, it is one of the biggest stadiums in the world.

Lights along the top of the roof

STANDING TALLER
Barcelona, Spain, moved from Les Corts Stadium to the spectacular Nou Camp in 1957. Improvements for the 1982 World Cup and 1992 Olympics have increased the staggering height of the stands. The Nou Camp was paid for by the club's members.

PATH TO THE PITCH
The tunnel is more than just a route on to the pitch. It is the place where players psyche themselves up for the game and give in to their superstitions. Many insist on taking the same place in the line every time. Others put on their shirts only at the last moment.

The roof "hangs" from this crossbar

The pylon is integral to the structure of the stand

KEEPING UP TO DATE
Modern stands are designed using computer models to ensure that everybody has a good view. The space between seats is a difficult issue. More space means greater comfort, but it reduces the capacity of the stand. Designs, such as faces, are often picked out in the seats.

FANS ON THEIR FEET
Before all-seater stadiums were introduced, fans stood packed together on terraces. Far more fans could get in to watch a match and it is how the majority of people have watched games for much of football's history. Children were often passed over the heads of the crowd to the front to give them a better view.

STATE OF THE ART
The Stade de France is in St Denis, north of Paris. It was built for the 1998 World Cup and 80,000 spectators watched the opening game there between Brazil and Scotland. The stadium was widely praised for its dramatic design. The roof, enclosing the ground in a continuous curve, creates an amphitheatre effect, which has always been popular in European and South American stadiums.

Several tiers of seats

Pitch level openings for emergency vehicles

Revolving advertizing hoardings around the pitch

The World Cup

THE FOOTBALL WORLD CUP is one of the greatest sporting events of our time. The first World Cup was held in Uruguay in 1930, 26 years after FIFA first discussed the idea. In the early days, some teams were unable to travel to the host country but, by the 1950s, long-distance travel was becoming much easier and quicker. As the tournament became more accessible, it grew in popularity. The 1950 World Cup final at the Maracana Stadium in Rio de Janeiro was attended by 200,000 people. In 1958, Brazilian teenager Pele became the first global football superstar. Since then, interest in the World Cup has boomed.

MANY MASCOTS
Every World Cup since 1966 has had a mascot. They appear as a life-size figure at matches and scaled-down promotional or commercial images. This is Pique, from Mexico '86.

WORLD FIRST
Uruguay offered to pay travel and accommodation expenses to the 13 visiting teams at the first World Cup. Only four European teams made the long journey, joining the seven South American teams.

1954 – Switzerland. West Germany beat Hungary 3–2 in one of the great upsets in World Cup history.

1958 – Sweden. Brazil beat Sweden 5–2. Brazil are the only team to have played in every Finals tournament.

1950 – Brazil. Uruguay beat Brazil 2–1, in the first tournament after the Second World War.

1962 – Chile. Brazil beat Czechoslovakia 3–1, with Garrincha taking centre stage after Pele was injured.

1938 – France. Italy beat Hungary 4–2, inspired by their star inside-forward, Meazza.

1966 – England. West Germany lost 2–4 to England in extra time, with Geoff Hurst scoring the first hat-trick in a final.

1934 – Italy. Czechoslovakia lost 1–2 to Italy. Uruguay did not defend their crown, the only time this has happened.

1970 – Mexico. Brazil beat Italy 4–1 and were one of the greatest teams of all time.

1930 – Uruguay. Beating Argentina 4–2, Uruguay was the first of many host countries to win the Cup.

1974 – West Germany. Holland were beaten 2–1 by West Germany, who came back from being a goal behind.

VARIOUS VENUES
Competition to stage the World Cup Finals is always fierce because it brings visitors and publicity to the host country. The Finals in 2002, in Japan and South Korea, will be the first shared tournament and the first to be held outside Europe and the Americas.

Argentina '78 is remembered for the ticker-tape in the River Plate Stadium

Mexico was the first country to host two Finals

The Italia '90 mascot was called Ciao

1978 – Argentina. Holland lost 1–3 to Argentina, leaving the Dutch as the best team never to have won the World Cup.

1982 – Spain. Italy beat West Germany 3–1, their striker Paolo Rossi finishing as leading scorer.

1986 – Mexico. Argentina beat West Germany 3–2, in a tournament dominated by Diego Maradona.

1990 – Italy. West Germany beat Argentina 1–0 in a defensive, bad-tempered final.

1998 – France. Brazil were beaten 3–0 by France in an amazingly one-sided match.

1994 – USA. Brazil beat Italy 3–2 on penalties after a 0–0 draw and became the only team to have won four World Cups.

The figure is a winged seraphim

WANDERING TROPHY
The first World Cup trophy was designed by a French sculptor, Abel Lafleur. It was later named in honour of the president of FIFA, Jules Rimet. The trophy was stolen before the 1966 tournament in England and was found in a park by a dog called Pickles. Brazil were presented with the trophy to keep in 1970 but it was stolen again and has not been seen since.

The engraving on the trophy is in French

The trophy is made of solid gold

COUPE DU MONDE DE FOOTBALL ASSOCIATION COUPE JULES RIMET

Jules Rimet trophy

In 1994, American fans turned out in force to watch the matches

The fans at Italia '90 provided more drama than some of the matches

Sweden, the host team, made it to the final in 1958 but were overpowered by the Brazilian super-team

READ ALL ABOUT IT
Programmes for the World Cup are different from the club variety, in that they usually cover the whole tournament rather than a specific match. They contain information about the competing teams and are printed in several languages. These programmes are from Sweden '58, England '66, Spain '82, Italy '90, and USA '94.

Didi

Pele was 17 in 1958

Garrincha

Vava played at centre-forward

Zagalo, the left-winger, scored the fourth goal in the final

THE BEAUTIFUL GAME
The 1958 final saw Brazil emerge as one of the World Cup's greatest-ever teams. Their forward line-up was among the strongest in the game's history. Garrincha, Didi, Vava, Pele, and Zagalo drove the team to victory. Mario Zagalo later became the national team manager and was in charge when Brazil won again in 1970 and 1994.

Continued on next page

WE MUST HAVE THE WORLD CUP
This was the poster for the 1962 Finals in Chile. A series of earthquakes marred the run-up to the tournament but the hosts were determined. President of the Chilean FA, Carlos Dittborn, said "We have nothing. That is why we must have the World Cup." Chile overcame the doubts of some European teams by staging a successful event. There was more trouble on the pitch than off it, particularly in the "Battle of Santiago" between Italy and Chile. Italy finished the game with nine men.

Globe forms the top of the trophy

World Cup Willie inspired a World Cup theme song by Lonnie Donnegan

The Union Jack flag represents Great Britain, not just England

Designed by Italian Silvio Gazzaniga, the trophy is made of solid 18-carat gold

The real trophy is 50.8 cm (20 in) high and weighs 9 kg (20 lbs)

Replica of the World Cup trophy

World Cup Willie was a lion, inspired by the three lions on the England kit

MASCOTS FOR MONEY
World Cup Willie was the first World Cup mascot. Designed for the 1966 tournament in England, he represented the increase in commercialism. Since then tournament mascots, such as Ciao of Italy '90 and Footix of France '98, have appeared on official posters and been sold in many forms.

NEW LOOK CUP
The present World Cup trophy was made for the 1974 Finals in West Germany. Having won for the third time in 1970, Brazil had been allowed to keep the Jules Rimet trophy for good. The new trophy was commissioned by FIFA, despite an offer from Brazil to provide a trophy named after FIFA president, Sir Stanley Rous.

Argentina '78

THINKING POSITIVE
In 1978, hosts Argentina inspired their passionate fans with their positive attitude. The star of their winning team was Mario Kempes who played club football in Europe.

WorldCup USA 94

SEE REVERSE SIDE FOR TERMS AND CONDITIONS

ENTHUSIASTIC AMERICA
Despite having no strong tradition of professional football, the USA hosted a successful World Cup Finals in 1994. Large and enthusiastic crowds attended all the games. This is a ticket for the game between Italy and Mexico, played at the former RFK Stadium, now the Jack Kent Cooke Stadium, home to American football team the Washington Redskins.

A pack of cards illustrating the stadiums

Spanish Football Federation crest

HARD WORK FOR HOSTS
A country bids to hold the World Cup several years in advance. They try to convince FIFA that they will be able to stage a successful tournament. They have to produce information about all aspects of the tournament, including the stadiums, transport networks, accommodation, and media facilities.

Fabien Barthez, France

Ronaldo, Brazil

Lilian Thuram, France

The balls are brightly coloured for the benefit of TV audiences

Each ball contains a slip of paper with a team written on it

WHO PLAYS WHO?
Plastic balls like these are used to make the draw for the World Cup Finals. It is a fair way to decide who plays who. The number of competing teams has steadily increased from 13 in 1930 to 32 in 1998. The present system ensures that every team gets to play three games in the first round. Then, for the rest of the tournament, games are played on a knock-out basis, until only two remain for the grand final.

IN THE BAG
This bag is a promotional item for the 2002 World Cup, to be staged jointly by Japan and South Korea. This will be the first shared tournament and the first to be held in Asia. Demand is sure to increase for smaller countries to benefit from this arrangement.

FRANCE IN ACTION
Brazil were expected to retain their title in 1998 but doubts surrounding Ronaldo's fitness to play seemed to distract them in the final. The goalkeeper Fabien Barthez was one of many members in the victorious French team who enhanced his reputation with a brilliant performance throughout the tournament.

Cups and trophies

THE MOMENT WHEN a team captain is presented with a trophy and holds it up to the fans is the crowning glory of any campaign. Cups and trophies are the marks of success and the managers of many modern clubs know that, if they are to hold on to their job, their team has to win a competition. For clubs like Real Madrid in Spain, Benfica in Portugal, and Bayern Munich in Germany, finishing as runners up is considered a failure. The desire to make money has led to the creation of many new competitions in recent years, some of which do not have the same prestige as older tournaments such as the European Cup or the Copa America.

OLYMPIC FOOTBALL
This badge is from the 1956 Olympic Games. The Olympics featured demonstration football matches from 1896. The first proper Olympic tournament was in 1908.

TEAM TALK
The European Cup was originally for the champions of each country's league. Now the top two clubs compete. The competition was first held in 1956. At the 1985 final at the Heysel Stadium in Brussels, Belgium, 39 people died. A safety wall collapsed as fans of Juventus, Italy and Liverpool, England fought each other.

Programme for the 1985 European Cup final

Corner flags used as decoration

EARLY CUP
This decorative, silver-plated trophy from the 1870s is an example of an early football cup. After the FA Cup was started in 1872, local tournaments for small clubs began to be set up all over England and Scotland along the same lines.

FULL HOUSE
In the 1999 Women's World Cup in the USA, teams played in front of capacity crowds. The final was held in the Rose Bowl in Passadena, California. Here, US player Cindy Parlow rides a tackle in the final against China. The USA won, to secure their second World Cup victory.

WOMENS' WORLD CUP
The first Women's World Cup took place in China in 1991. The final was held in Guangzhou, where the USA beat Norway 2–1. The tournament went from strength to strength and the next two events, in 1995 and 1999, drew large crowds. This is the trophy awarded to the USA in 1999.

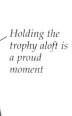

The gold-plated Women's World Cup trophy has a football at the top

Holding the trophy aloft is a proud moment

PLAYER'S CIGARETTES | **PLAYER'S CIGARETTES**

ASSOCIATION CUP WINNERS
THE OLD CUP

ASSOCIATION CUP W
THE PRESENT CUP

LITTLE TIN IDOLS
The first FA Cup, on the left, was known as the Little Tin Idol. It was stolen from a shop display in 1895 and was never recovered. The present FA Cup, on the right, was made in Bradford, England, in 1912.

The silver UEFA trophy is decorated with men playing football

Names of previous winners engraved around the base

FROM STRENGTH TO STRENGTH
The African Nations Cup has been held every two years since 1957. It has grown from humble beginnings and as many as 16 teams now take part. Egyptian striker Hassan Hossam is pictured here after his team's 1998 triumph over the defending champions, South Africa. This was Egypt's fourth African Nations title.

COPA AMERICA CUP
First held in 1910, the Copa America is the oldest major international competition. It was originally played for only by South American countries but, in recent years, Mexico and the USA have also taken part. Uruguay won the first official Copa America in 1917 and, along with Argentina, have been the most successful teams over the years. Brazil have not always played their strongest team. Since 1987, the tournament has been held every two years.

SECOND BEST
The UEFA (Union of European Football Associations) Cup was originally known as the Inter City Fairs Cup. The first competition was played over three years, beginning in 1955. Barcelona beat London 8–2 in the two-legged final. When the European Cup Winner's Cup was abolished in 1999, only two European club competitions remained. The strongest sides qualify for the European Cup and the next best play in the UEFA Cup.

The Copa America was conceived by Chile, Uruguay, Brazil, and Argentina

Playing the game

Two lead "kicking" figures from the early 20th century

GENERATIONS OF children have had their first contact with football through toys such as blow football, card games, and Subbuteo. The popularity of football means that, as with other merchandise, there is money to be made from developing new products with a football theme. This drives manufacturers and inventors to come up with a vast range of games based on football, far more than on any other sport. The simplicity of the toys from the past, shown here, contrasts sharply with the speed and excitement of modern computer games. Today, children and adults can experience virtual football games and act out the roles of their favourite players and teams on play stations and in computer games.

This game was advanced for its time

Points are lost if a marble is trapped here

Marbles are fired up this chute

BALL ROLLING
This hand-held toy was made in the early 20th century. It involves rolling the ball-bearing into one of the small holes.

IN THE TRENCHES
Trench Football was produced for British soldiers fighting in the First World War. The player must move a ball-bearing safely past the German generals to score.

FOOTBALL MATCHBOX
This is the world's smallest football game, probably made in Japan in the 1930s for small children. When the matchbox is opened, a spring is released and the players leap up.

PINBALL
In this bagatelle game from the 1950s, players shoot marbles around the board using a spring in the bottom right-hand corner. Points are scored or lost according to where the marbles stop.

Ball for the Kick game

The cards feature different positions and parts of the match

Downward pressure on one leg causes the other leg to kick

KICK FIGURES

These figures come from a table-top game called Kick, made in about 1900. A green cloth pitch, and goals with nets are included. Players make the mechanical footballers kick by pressing them down on the table. They are moved around by hand – a feature also used in more modern football toys.

Combination of red and white is a classic football strip

Key fits into the ball to wind it up

SNAP!

This rare pack of snap cards from the early 20th century features football characters. In snap, players aim to collect all the cards. They turn over cards until two identical ones turn up together. The first player to shout "Snap!" takes the pile.

CLOCKWORK PLAYER

This tin-plate clockwork toy was made in Germany in the early 1950s. When wound up with a key, the figure moves forwards, as if dribbling the ball. The shirt, with its loosely laced neck, is typical of the style of football clothes worn in Europe at that time.

CHAMPIONS!

This game, called Championship Soccer, was made in 1983. It uses two of the classic components of many board games – dice and cards – to govern the movement of the ball around the field. A scoreboard and clock are also included.

QUICK CHANGE

These wooden blocks, with a different picture on each side, can be jumbled up to make a character. The shin-pads and ball reflect the style of the time when the toy was made – 1895.

Memorabilia

F OOTBALL appeals to all parts of the community, regardless of age or sex. The game can therefore be used to promote a wide range of items. Football-related advertising and product promotion is not a new phenomenon. In fact, companies were already latching on to the game's popularity in the early part of the 20th century. An understated style and original artwork predominated until the 1950s. This has been largely replaced today by mass-produced items, heavily reliant on star players and wealthy clubs.

1910 Silver Vesta (match holder) advertising the mustard maker Colman's

Bank Top White Star

Wednesday, now Sheffield Wednesday

Welsh national team

Chadderton, a non-league team

Scottish club, Hearts

BAINES CARDS
These cards, produced in the early 20th century, were the forerunners of sticker albums and other collectibles. They featured football and rugby league teams at professional and amateur level and had advertisements on the reverse side.

SPORTS TIN
By the 1930s, original artwork on a sporting theme was often used as a decoration for everyday household items. This tin features football on the lid and other sports, including cricket and hockey, around the outside.

Covered stands are rare in southern Europe

FIFA logo for Italia '90

SOUVENIRS
Mementoes of the World Cup Finals do not stop at programmes and tickets. There is great demand around the world for anything tied to the tournament, such as these erasers from Italia '90.

FOOTBALL FAN
This is a Spanish lady's fan from the mid 20th century, printed in Barcelona. It has a football image on one side and carries a promotional message on the reverse. Many commercial objects of this period were designed to be artistic as well as functional.

POSTER PAINTING
In this advertising card of the 1920s, an Italian drinks company have illustrated their product in a football scene, instead of putting a football image on the actual bottle.

HEALTHY KICK
There is no magic ingredient in this drink, but the images would have appealed to football fans. The manufacturers knew that any association with football would improve sales.

This label comes from a fruity soft drink. It was marketed as an ideal refreshment for half-time

This label implies that the drink will promote the robust strength that a footballer enjoys

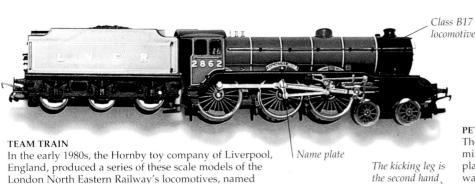

Class B17
locomotive

Name plate

Banks Johnstone Jennings England Best

TEAM TRAIN
In the early 1980s, the Hornby toy company of Liverpool, England, produced a series of these scale models of the London North Eastern Railway's locomotives, named after football clubs. This one is called the *Manchester United*. Real trains are also sometimes named after clubs.

PETROL HEADS
The Cleveland Petrol company produced these miniatures of British international players in 1971. The set was given away free with petrol sales.

The kicking leg is the second hand

Pocket watch

Watch

Alarm clock

Chain

FULL TIME
This group includes a Swiss pocket watch made in Geneva around 1910, a British watch from the 1950s, and a more modern 1970s alarm clock. Design, materials, and therefore cost were dictated by whether the object was aimed at children or adults.

CHAIN MEDALS
Football items are often turned into jewellery and other personal effects. Four silver medals, struck in the 1920s, are attached to this chain. The silver locket and compass are from the 1880s.

Locket

Compass

Further medals could be added to the chain

OLYMPIC CLOCK
This German wooden clock may well have been made to commemorate the 1936 Berlin Olympics, where the football tournament was won by Italy, when they beat Austria 2–1 in the final. The figures at the top of the clock move on the hour.

The figure is the same on both halves

SOAP ON A ROPE
The Avon company produced this soap football to mark the 1966 World Cup Finals in England.

STRING ALONG
Made in the 1880s, this copper string holder prevents string from getting tangled. The string is pulled through a hole in the top.

CHOCOLATE
Melted chocolate would have been poured into this early 20th century brass mould and left to cool and set, producing a miniature chocolate footballer with a ball at his feet. This item was made to appeal mainly to children and the general footballing theme would have been enough to make it popular.

The business of football

FOOTBALL IS BIG BUSINESS – fans attend matches in large numbers, club products sell worldwide, and top players and managers earn an incredibly large wage. The people who started professionalism in the 1880s realized the financial possibilities of football but, for many decades, the game carried on at much the same level. It provided cheap entertainment for the paying public and offered a decent living to players and managers. All that has changed now, as club owners and star players stretch football's money-making potential to the limit.

Gullit, pictured here in a pre-season friendly, occasionally played for the teams he was managing as player-manager

The emblem of the sponsoring local brewery

BILLY'S BRIBE
This shirt was worn by Welshman Billy Meredith, the greatest player of his era. He was one of several Manchester City, England, players who were banned from playing for a year in 1905. They allegedly tried to bribe the Aston Villa captain £10 to lose an important game. This was the first major scandal of British football.

GETTING SHIRTY
Replica shirts are a major source of income for professional clubs like England's Manchester United or Spain's Real Madrid. Three or four designs are now available at one time and new ones are brought out at regular intervals. Clubs produce hundreds of different products – from calenders to baby clothes; from sweets to bicycles. These can be sold to fans all over the world, reducing the club's reliance on gate receipts.

MANAGEMENT STRESS
Managers are subjected to great stress in the modern game and have to accept that their every decision will be examined by the media. In most of the major leagues, the length of time allowed for a manager to produce a winning team can be measured in months rather than years. In 1999, Ruud Gullit was forced out of his job as manager at England's Newcastle United after just a few unsuccessful months.

Even shin-pads, worn under the socks, are marked with the name of the manufacturer

SHIRT ADVERT
In the 1970s, businesses began to pay for the right to advertize on team kits. Within a few years, even non-league teams had some income from this source. Pictured here are Fernando Redondo of Real Madrid, Spain, and Paolo Sousa of Inter Milan, Italy, sporting their sponsor's logos.

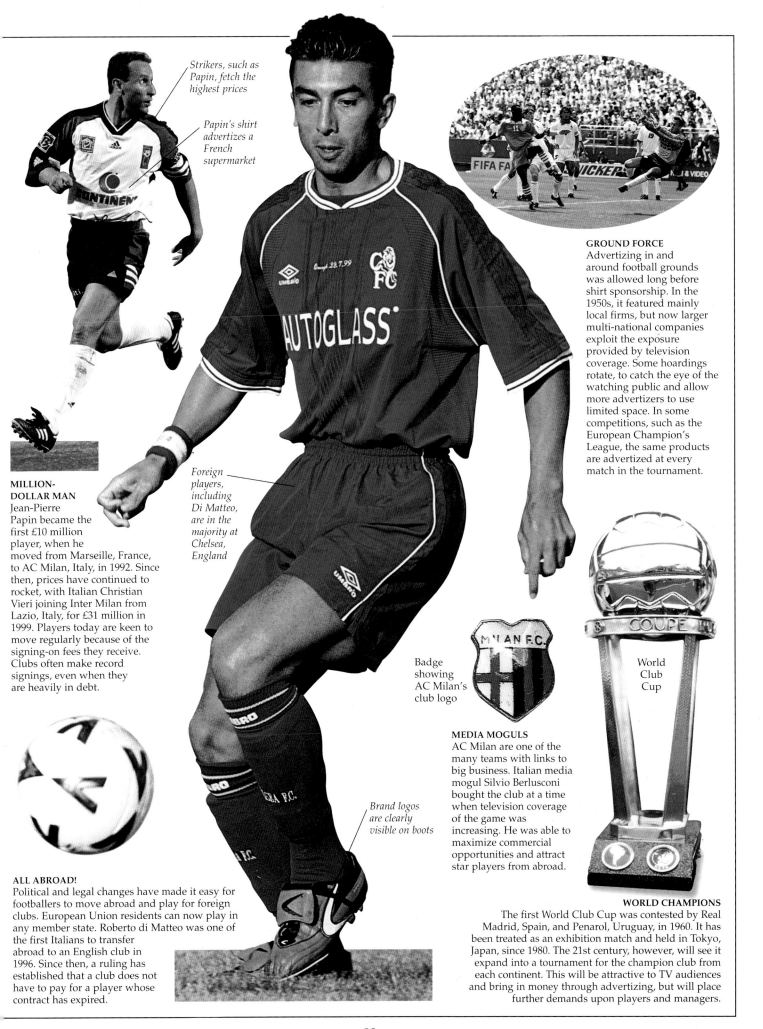

Strikers, such as Papin, fetch the highest prices

Papin's shirt advertizes a French supermarket

GROUND FORCE

Advertizing in and around football grounds was allowed long before shirt sponsorship. In the 1950s, it featured mainly local firms, but now larger multi-national companies exploit the exposure provided by television coverage. Some hoardings rotate, to catch the eye of the watching public and allow more advertizers to use limited space. In some competitions, such as the European Champion's League, the same products are advertized at every match in the tournament.

MILLION-DOLLAR MAN

Jean-Pierre Papin became the first £10 million player, when he moved from Marseille, France, to AC Milan, Italy, in 1992. Since then, prices have continued to rocket, with Italian Christian Vieri joining Inter Milan from Lazio, Italy, for £31 million in 1999. Players today are keen to move regularly because of the signing-on fees they receive. Clubs often make record signings, even when they are heavily in debt.

Foreign players, including Di Matteo, are in the majority at Chelsea, England

Badge showing AC Milan's club logo

World Club Cup

MEDIA MOGULS

AC Milan are one of the many teams with links to big business. Italian media mogul Silvio Berlusconi bought the club at a time when television coverage of the game was increasing. He was able to maximize commercial opportunities and attract star players from abroad.

Brand logos are clearly visible on boots

ALL ABROAD!

Political and legal changes have made it easy for footballers to move abroad and play for foreign clubs. European Union residents can now play in any member state. Roberto di Matteo was one of the first Italians to transfer abroad to an English club in 1996. Since then, a ruling has established that a club does not have to pay for a player whose contract has expired.

WORLD CHAMPIONS

The first World Club Cup was contested by Real Madrid, Spain, and Penarol, Uruguay, in 1960. It has been treated as an exhibition match and held in Tokyo, Japan, since 1980. The 21st century, however, will see it expand into a tournament for the champion club from each continent. This will be attractive to TV audiences and bring in money through advertizing, but will place further demands upon players and managers.

Index

Acknowledgments

Dorling Kindersley would like to thank:
Hugh Hornby, Rob Pratten, and Lynsey Jones at the Football Museum for their help and patience.

The publishers would also like to thank the following for their kind permission to reproduce their photographs:

a=above; c=centre; b=below; l=left; r=right; t=top; f=far; n=near;

Action Plus: 58bl; Glyn Kirk 15l, 18tr, 18cl, 18br, 19tl, 23cr, 44br, 51bl, 58clb; Matthew Clarke 19c; Neil Tingle 12br.
Allsport: 34cl, 34br, 35tl, 35c; Ben Radford 58cr; Christopher Guibbaud 59tl; Claudio Villa 18bl; Clive Brunskill 16bl; David Cannon 19c, 53cr; David Leah 53c; Don Morley 18br; Hulton Getty 36bl; Jed Jacbsohn 52c; Michael Cooper 59c; Michael King 36-7bc; Scott R Indermaur 45tl; Vincent Laforet 52br.
Bryan Horsnell: 44cl, 44cfl, 44cnl.
Colorsport: 13tr, 21r, 23br, 29tr, 30tr, 34bl, 41tr, 46-7 b, 59tr; Jerome Provost 41bc; Olympia 36br, 37tr.
Corbis UK Ltd: S Carmona 46clb.
Empics Ltd: 34tnr; Don Morley 37tr; Michael Steele 43bl, 43br; Neale Simpson 40cl; Peter Robinson 36tc, 49l, 59br; Tony Marshall 19bl; Topham Picturepoint 36bc, 37tl; Witters 34tr.
Hulton Getty: 19bl, 35cr, 35bl, 36tl.
Mark Leech: 45bl.
Popperfoto: 53cl.
Sporting Pictures (uk) Ltd: 4cr, 24cl, 25tl, 25tr, 33br, 38bl, 46cl.

Jacket
Allsport: front cl; Graham Chadwick back bl; Gary M Prior back cl; Ben Radford front cr.
Bryan Horsnell: back cb, back cbl, back tc, back cbr, front tc.
Colorsport: back br, back cla.
Mary Evans Picture Library: spine, front tcr.
The Robert Opie Collection: back tfl, back tfl, front tr.

DK EYEWITNESS GUIDES

SUBJECTS

HISTORY
AFRICA
ARMS & ARMOUR
BATTLE
CASTLE
CHINA
COWBOY
EXPLORER
KNIGHT
MEDIEVAL LIFE
MYTHOLOGY
NORTH AMERICAN INDIAN
PIRATE
PRESIDENTS
RUSSIA
SHIPWRECK
TITANIC
VIKING
WITCH & WIZARD

ANCIENT WORLDS
ANCIENT EGYPT
ANCIENT GREECE
ANCIENT ROME
AZTEC
BIBLE LANDS
MUMMY
PYRAMID

THE BEGINNINGS OF LIFE
ARCHAEOLOGY
DINOSAUR
EARLY PEOPLE
PREHISTORIC LIFE

THE ARTS
CINEMA
COSTUME
DANCE
MUSIC
WRITING

TECHNOLOGY
BOAT
CAR
FLYING MACHINE
FUTURE
INVENTION
SPACE EXPLORATION
TRAIN

PAINTING
GOYA
IMPRESSIONISM
LEONARDO
MANET
MONET
PERSPECTIVE
RENAISSANCE
VAN GOGH
WATERCOLOUR

SCIENCE

ASTRONOMY

CHEMISTRY

EARTH

ECOLOGY

ELECTRICITY

ELECTRONICS

ENERGY

EVOLUTION

FORCE & MOTION

HUMAN BODY

LIFE

LIGHT

MATTER

MEDICINE

SKELETON

TECHNOLOGY

TIME & SPACE

SPORT

AMERICAN FOOTBALL

BASEBALL

FOOTBALL

OLYMPICS

SPORT

ANIMALS

AMPHIBIAN

BIRD

BUTTERFLY & MOTH

CAT

DOG

EAGLE

ELEPHANT

FISH

GORILLA

HORSE

INSECT

MAMMAL

REPTILE

SHARK

WHALE

HABITATS

ARCTIC & ANTARCTIC

DESERT

JUNGLE

OCEAN

POND & RIVER

SEASHORE

THE EARTH

CRYSTAL & GEM

FOSSIL

HURRICANE & TORNADO

PLANT

ROCK & MINERAL

SHELL

TREE

VOLCANO

WEATHER

THE WORLD AROUND US

BUILDING

CRIME & DETECTION

FARM

FLAG

MEDIA

MONEY

RELIGION

SPY

Future updates and editions will be available online at www.dk.com

DK EYEWITNESS GUIDES

A–Z

Future updates and editions will be available online at www.dk.com